PATH TO THE LIGHT

Kabbalah Centre Publishing is a registered DBA of Kabbalah Centre International, Inc.

For further information:

The Kabbalah Centre
155 E. 48th St., New York, NY 10017
1062 S. Robertson Blvd., Los Angeles, CA 90035

1.800.Kabbalah www.kabbalah.com

Printed in USA, July 2017

ISBN: 978-1-57189-963-7

Design: HL Design (Hyun Min Lee) www.hldesignco.com

PATH TO THE LIGHT

DECODING THE BIBLE WITH KABBALAH

An Anthology
of Commentary
from Kabbalist
Rav Berg

**BOOK OF
BERESHEET
Volume 1**

Beresheet
Noah
Lech Lecha

Thank You Rav.

Love,
Esther

PREFACE

Here, for the first time, is Rav Berg's commentary on the Bible, assembled from talks and lectures given over the past forty years to students on three continents. Because the commentary collates transcriptions of material given under vastly differing conditions, over an enormous period of time, we have had to edit scrupulously, avoiding gratuitous repetitions but preserving the subtle nuances and additional insights the Rav can bring in when discussing the same subject on different occasions. In turning his speech into prose, we have striven to preserve his inimitable style, humor, passion, and fondness for jokes or analogies—pertinent to the time he delivered them—that suddenly bring a complex proposition into startlingly simple clarity. If we have not succeeded, the fault is ours, not his.

This is no mere explanation of the Torah. You will not find a textual exegesis of Genesis, Exodus, Numbers, Leviticus and Deuteronomy—as the books are named in English translations—but instead a profound discussion on their inner and coded meanings, and what their relevance is to us today. This is, in essence, the heart of Kabbalah, to the teaching of which the Rav devoted his life. As it has always been, his purpose here is to give instruction on how people can improve their everyday lives, attain a state of wisdom, and reach the kind of peace and tranquility that is applicable to the world here and now. As the Rav often says, this is not a religion, and not about worshipping an unknowable God—it is pragmatic information.

There are, of course, countless references to and quotations from the Zohar, the Talmud, Rav Isaac Luria (the Ari), Rashi, and many other kabbalists and biblical commentators, spanning three millennia. But in dealing with the plethora of extremely difficult passages, puzzling Divine injunctions, unfathomable events or perplexing statements in the Bible, the Rav will frequently summon up familiar themes to link these ancient books to what he teaches in the late 20th and early 21st centuries about dealing with the vicissitudes of daily life. Just as we find the concept of space, time, motion, and the Flawless Universe in a discussion of the Days of Creation, we find the security shield and an astrological meditation on Scorpio, as well as a disquisition on the nature of water used to unravel the story of Noah.

The Rav's scope of reference is extraordinary. He will go from parallels with modern particle or astrophysics to environmental sciences, and then to events from history and even pre-history. Yet always his intention is to elucidate, to show us what the Bible has to tell us today. As it is with many great sages, he is, on a few occasions at least, far ahead of his time, and such ideas may not be fully understood for many decades to come. When the Rav talks of Kabbalah expounding a 23rd or even a 25th century science, he is not joking. Those ideas that may seem hopelessly complicated or foreign to us now, with serious contemplation and questioning, help us to expand our consciousness. For the Rav's intention is to provide us with information of value, not to confound us. Helping us understand that there is no new knowledge discovered, but rather infinite wisdom that has always existed, waiting to be revealed. Our ability to travel back in time, for example, is a genuine reality and tool for *tikkun*, the spiritual correction that is the purpose of life on Earth. It merely needs a conscious awareness of it to benefit from it.

If there is a single overall message in these commentaries, it is that the Bible is written in a code. These are not old narratives about people long ago. The stories are representative of the spiritual energy and wisdom that supports and revisits humanity as long as we traverse this physical dimension. Readers will find this to be a recurrent theme throughout the following commentaries.

Another theme is the importance of the Hebrew language and the *Alef Bet*, which cannot be exaggerated. Usually a topic for philologists or scholars of semantics, here, however, the Hebrew words and their translations are presented in simple, cogent terms that illuminate problematical verses as dramatically as if someone had switched on a light in the dark. So engaged in his mission of elucidation is the Rav that he will use any device of memory or knowledge to open up his subject for the ordinary reader, be it anecdotes from his family history or the principals of electrical engineering. As he explains the Three Column System by analogy to the positive and negative poles whose current is restricted by a filament to produce light, we see, as it is developed over many talks, the brilliance of this. Each time the Rav returns to a similar device, he builds upon it, identifying further subtleties we have not previously noticed, and which have a peculiar application to the text under discussion.

Readers will also find here, in sequence, the portions in their English translation. This is an editorial instrument that allowed us to provide you, the reader, with a framework to learn from all that the Rav had said over 40 years about the portion. For those who were blessed to have attended those lectures, this will provide a lasting testimonial to the revolution that the Rav established with his wisdom and exceptional gifts as a teacher. For those who did not, it is an uplifting record of unequalled spiritual pedagogy—for the Rav was truly the kabbalist for this generation, and the world's teacher.

Kabbalah Centre Publishing

Table of Contents

INTRODUCTION BY RAV BERG

The Book of Beresheet contains so many stories that it can read like a collection of fairy tales. However, the Zohar tells us that anyone who thinks the Bible is just a series of yarns about people three millennia ago is a fool—better they had never been born. What does the Zohar mean by such an uncharitable statement? If we see the Bible as merely stories then we miss the opportunity to live. When there is existence without life, it is better to not have been born at all.

In the Book of Beresheet we are given wisdom about how to live in this physical world. From Abraham, we learn how to truly care about others. From Isaac, we learn how to discern. And from Jacob, we learn to be honest. As it is written: "Give truth to Jacob and loving-kindness to Abraham." (Micha: 7:20)

These biblical accounts are meant to raise our consciousness, opening our eyes so they see at last. When we truly see, we are finally able to face the difficult issues that humanity has experienced in the same way, since the beginning of time. The circumstances are different, to be sure, but the lessons are unchanging. If we read the Bible without opening our eyes, it can seem merely like a simplistic history lesson—things that happened to a people living long, long ago. Instead, these biblical tales are meant to provide a guide to help us understand the eternal question of our soul's real purpose here.

The Zohar also tells us that, while studying the Bible helps us to awaken our consciousness, it is the reading of the Torah Scroll on Shabbat that removes chaos. Without the knowledge given to us by the Zohar, we can often find this reading to be a burdensome, time-consuming, "religious" activity. The Zohar says that the Torah is the road to the Tree of Life Reality, the path to the removal of chaos.

Rav Shimon bar Yochai, 2nd century sage and author of the Zohar, explains that most people who participate in a Shabbat service will walk out empty because they are not fully aware of the purpose of attending this service in the first place. The purpose of attending Shabbat is not to feel good—although there is nothing wrong with feeling good, but this is not the true purpose of attending it.

There are five Books of Moses. Why five and not four or three? It is not due to the availability of ink; nor does it contain all there is to be said on many issues. Such reasoning relates only to the physical manifestation of so great a spiritual document. The number five refers to the five bottled-up energies of which this world consists: Keter, Chochmah, Binah, Zeir Anpin, and Malchut.

From Rav Shimon we learn that the Torah is a channel, and it is also considered to be an instrument, a technology designed to take us, in a very precise way, back in time. There are those who believe it is impossible to go back in time—because, if we could do so, it would mean the existence of a speed greater than that of light. However, if we cannot go back in time, it means everything that has ever been is forever stationary in our lives. If this is true, how can we ever expect to erase the past that governs our future? How can we change what is to come if we cannot go back and expunge some of the past that now governs the future as part of our *tikkun*—the reincarnation process? How can we expect to ever to achieve a better life, based on the errors of previous incarnations and our present transgressions, if our future is determined by the past? Rav Shimon concludes that there is a way out of this dilemma—even though there may not appear to be one.

Furthermore, if we have already charted the course of our future due to negative actions performed in the past, then what is the sense of coming back again at all? If a prior lifetime also includes the present lifetime, and if the present lifetime is included in the past, nothing would ever change. In other words, when I plant an apple seed, I know what fruit will come to me in a few years because the potential is included within the seed itself. The Zohar tells us that the instrument called the Torah can provide a means by which we can turn back the past. It is the only method we have at our disposal that will do so, week after week.

The coming week is included in the past, and it can be changed by going back into the past before the next week begins. If we can somehow erase actions of the past week, then the past will no longer govern a future that is otherwise destined to include chaos. The purpose of reading the Torah is to bring us back to the past. But it is only sufficient to bring us back one week and cover the seven days that follow. This, in itself, however, is a gift we are blessed to have been given. If we hear but one Torah reading in a year, then, at least, for that one week, we can experience the breath of freedom. For the Torah to accomplish the important job of returning us back in time, there must be a proper vehicle to transport us. This means that the Scroll has to be valid, and there needs to be an aware and awakened consciousness in the listener. In other words, just listening to the reading and not understanding what it is we can achieve through that reading is an exercise in futility. Knowledge is the connection. This is a key principle of Kabbalah.

It is explained in Beresheet 4: "Adam knew Eve and she became pregnant." There seems to be a lack of logic here. Is the Bible merely being polite? The Zohar explains that "knowing" is the code word for an energy-intelligence. The act of unifying a male and a female can produce life. It is a profound connection of energies that can generate and power a human being. From this, the Zohar concludes that, when the Bible says Adam "knew" Eve, we are to understand that it is knowledge that makes the connection. Those who do not "know" have not connected.

I would like to conclude this introduction with a discussion on the subject of appreciation. It is a life's work to realize and comprehend the Bible's importance in our lives. When we hear the reading of the Torah Scroll, we are putting an end to that which has only brought pain, suffering, and chaos for untold centuries. When we appreciate, we begin to realize that we are not totally capable of controlling and mastering our destiny by ourselves alone. According to the Zohar, appreciation is not expressing our "thank you" but rather, having appreciation is a means by which we can receive. Just as knowledge is the connection, appreciation is the reception. The Zohar tells us that appreciation is, in reality, an act designed to benefit us, ourselves. The following commentary on the Book of Beresheet is therefore designed to elicit in readers a profound appreciation for the depth and wisdom of the Bible hidden within its coded language. This wisdom is, in turn, conferred upon the reader, whose appreciation for it is thus transformed into an inestimable benefit that, it is to be hoped, will enhance and transfigure a lifetime.

—Compiled from Lectures by Rav Berg

BOOK OF BERESHEET:

Portion of Beresheet

PORTION OF BERESHEET

The Truth about Creation

Over the past three to four thousand years, there has been a total misconception of Creation. The reason I say this is that, if Kabbalah had been available to everyone, there would be a different interpretation of how the world began. Until Kabbalah, I never understood the conflict between religion and science, and the theories that emerged on either side, as scholarship progressed and everyone came up with their own theory of the Big Bang or the origin of the universe.

In all of this, the simplest matter has been ignored—and science generally deals with the simple very poorly. The ample evidence of dinosaur skeletons shows us that dinosaurs once existed. Yet, the Zohar says nothing becomes extinct, everything that has ever lived is still present in some form. The great dinosaurs are still with us, except they have evolved and become reduced into reptiles. Adam and Eve were giants—Adam could reach into the Heavens. He was no more afraid of dinosaurs than we are afraid of lizards today. Yet fundamentalist religion ignores the simple truth that dinosaurs existed. The simple truth has been disregarded and, as a consequence, we have to face the resulting chaos. The Hebrew Bible makes the truth so clear but we cannot interpret it literally. The key is simplicity. It is not possible to translate the Bible because it is a code, and the key to breaking this code is the Zohar.

If yesterday, tomorrow, and today are preordained, it would seem that there is no free will. This is why it is said that God created darkness, so that there would be Bread of Shame—which gives us the freedom to choose between good and evil.

Beresheet is an opportunity to make contact with a new life. The wisest of all men—those who are truly wise, not superficially wise like us—know that everything that will happen has already happened. So is there no free will? Our choice is to live in goodness with the Tree of Life or in evil with the Tree of Knowledge. Within either alternative there is no true choice. When one is positioned with the Tree of Life, it is then said not to eat from the Tree of Knowledge because whoever is aligned with the Tree of Life should not connect with the Tree of Knowledge for even a moment. A genuine wise man knows he is a fool. I am vehement about staying aligned with the consciousness of the Tree of Life. People think that I am a *tzadik* but I do not side with the Tree of Life to be a *tzadik*—it is only because I know it is worth my while to cling to the Tree of Life for its goodness that I do so.

There are people who seek the Messiah because they think that when he comes, their life will change for the better—that the Messiah will end all problems—but this is a misconception. As it is written in the Zohar, in the portion of Shemot, when the Messiah comes, everyone will want to kill him. It is then that the problems will really begin for those who are not ready. Compared to the difficulties humankind will face then, this current chaos is still nothing. For this reason we must transform ourselves if we wish to bring Messiah with *rachamim* (the energy of mercy). If we do not, we will face major chaos, as it is written in the Zohar.

Beresheet 1:1 In the beginning God created the Heavens and the Earth.

Beresheet and the First Precept

We could devote a lifetime of study to the first seven days of Creation. The portion of Beresheet represents Keter and is more concealed than any other portion of the Bible. The purpose of studying Beresheet is to implant within ourselves both the understanding and the power of the very beginning, so that we can establish a closer connection to Keter (Crown). The more we are bonded with Keter—the more we are connected to the root—we will thereby have more influence. At the level of Keter everything is smaller in nature, like a seed or sperm. Once things evolve and develop, they are harder to change or control. For example, it is easier to manage a little seed by deciding where, when, and how you would like to plant it. But once the tree is fully grown in the ground, it is much more difficult to move or alter.

The first verse of Beresheet begins with the large Hebrew letter *Bet*. Many commentators ask why the first word of the first verse, of the first portion of the entire Bible begins with a large *Bet*? Why not another letter? And why a large letter, as opposed to a small or regular-sized letter? For the answers to these and other questions we turn to the Zohar, which says:

> "In the beginning, God created..." (Beresheet 1:1) This is the first and foremost precept of all. And this precept is called "the fear of God," which is called the "beginning." As it is written, "The fear of God is the beginning of wisdom;" (Tehilim 111:10) "The fear of God is the beginning of knowledge." (Mishlei 1:7). Because this fear (or awe) is called a beginning, and it is the gateway through which one

enters into Faith, based on this precept, the whole world is able to exist.
—Zohar, Prologue 21:189

In other words, the Zohar is saying that Beresheet 1:1, which states *Beresheet bara Elokim…*, is not discussing Creation, it is teaching us a precept. The word *resheet* comes from the word *yareh* (*Yud, Resh, Alef*), which means a "state of fear" and is therefore not referring to the word "beginning." Rather it is describing the concept of *yirat HaShem* or "fear of the Lord." This is certainly a departure from our original understanding. The Zohar explains that the whole world achieves its permanency on this first precept of the first verse in the Bible. In other words, if we do not have *yir'at HaShem* or "fear of God," the world cannot exist. From the above passage, it would seem that the Zohar begins with religiosity. However, we know the Zohar does not preach religion, so why does the Bible begin with fearing God?

The Zohar explains that to attain *chochmah* or "wisdom," requires *yir'at HaShem*. Yet how can we fear something of which we cannot conceive?

Those who have knowledge of the Hebrew language will recognize that the word *ro'eh* or "to see"—*Resh, Alef, Hei*—is constructed with the same three root letters found in the words *yir'ah* or *yareh*—*Yud, Resh, Alef, Hei*—which we have already stated means "to fear." The Zohar says if *resheet* is the code for *yirah* or "fear" and *ro'eh* is "seeing," then this fear and seeing is what created Heaven and Earth, and is what ensures the continued existence of the world of Heaven and Earth.

The Zohar continues:

> Fear is divided into three types. Two have no fundamental
> sources and one is the actual source of fear. There is a
> person who fears and respects the Holy One, blessed be He,
> so that his children will live and not die, or because he is
> afraid to be punished through his body or his wealth. This
> person, therefore, is always afraid of Him. But we can see
> that the fear he has of the Holy One, blessed be He, has
> no actual source, THAT IS, IS NOT FUNDAMENTALLY
> GENUINE, BECAUSE HIS OWN BENEFIT IS THE
> ROOT CAUSE, WHILE THE FEAR IS ONLY ITS
> RESULT. And there is a person who fears the Holy One,
> blessed be He, because he is afraid of the punishment that
> awaits him in the other world, and the tortures of *Gehenom*.
> These two KINDS OF FEAR, NAMELY THE FEAR
> OF PUNISHMENT A PERSON RECEIVES IN THIS
> WORLD AND THE FEAR OF THE PUNISHMENT
> IN THE WORLD TO COME, are not the essence of fear
> nor its genuine source.
> —Zohar, Prologue, 21:190

People fear God because they are afraid He can take away their life
or possessions. A president or a king can also elicit this kind of fear,
which, according to the Zohar, is not considered *resheet*. The root
of fearing a loss, or a leader in power, reveal but one concern—not
for the Lord, but for oneself. Rav Shimon makes it very clear that
self-preservation is not the essence of what we are discussing or its
genuine source.

> The fear (*resheet*) that is essential and genuine occurs when a
> person fears his Master because he is almighty and governs
> all; because He is the main source and essence of all worlds,
> and everything that exists is as nothing compared to Him.

As it is written, "and all the inhabitants of the Earth are reputed as nothing," (Daniel 4:32) and a person should concentrate his desires to that place that is called "fear."
—Zohar, Prologue 21:191

Fear of God is not a matter of perceiving God as a being to be reckoned with because He controls whether we will go to Heaven or Hell or live a life of poverty or wealth. Rav Shimon explains that fear of God means seeing and thereby understanding every aspect pertaining to ourselves and our relationship to the whole cosmos. When we reach the level of consciousness of *yir'at HaShem* and can see what the game of life is all about, as well as our place within the universe, we are able to control Heaven and Earth. While we are here, we are meant to rule the Heavens and the Earth.

Now we will go back to the question of why the Bible begins with a letter Bet. The Zohar says that the letter *Bet* is certainty, because, if everyone could see tomorrow, would there be uncertainty? Would the market crash be so terrible if we knew that everything would rise again the next day?

The reason the Bible begins with Bet is to reveal the *yir'ah* or the ability *to see*. The *Bet* has the power to create *bracha* or "blessing"—not, however, in the manner of *bless me now in the way I want things*, but rather *bless me to see things from beginning to end*. As most of us are limited by time, space, and motion, we can only perceive one day at a time. Things go up and down, and this is uncertainty—we are not sure what tomorrow will bring.

For those who can see the entire picture of the cosmos all at once, it will always be good, not only for themselves but for everyone else as well—this is *bracha* or "blessing." Therefore, the Torah Scroll begins with a *Bet*.

Why is this *Bet* large? There are three sizes of letters in the Torah Scroll: Large, regular, and small. The Zohar explains that the Torah is a cosmic code and the size of each letter also provides us with clues that help us to unlock its mysteries. The large *Bet* refers to Binah (the thought energy-intelligence of Understanding). This fits with the concept of *Beresheet* previously discussed: Certainty occurs when there is a consciousness of complete understanding.

When we understand the picture, not just for today but from beginning to end, we can see that there is *bracha*. We read the Torah, and connect with the large letter *Bet* to provide us with Binah consciousness so that we can be elevated above uncertainty—where there is no *bracha*—to the level where we see everything right from beginning to end. When we see everything, instantly and all at once, there is *bracha*.

The regular-sized letters connect to Zeir Anpin consciousness, and the small letters connect to Malchut consciousness. Malchut is the lowest level, with the least understanding, the least embodiment of energy-intelligence.

The Zohar explains that, within the portion of Beresheet, there is a Beresheet One and a Beresheet Two. In fact, there are two volumes of the Zohar just on the portion of Beresheet. This is why I say it would take seventy years to understand all of the implications that are involved in just this one verse.

We want to touch on the significance of Beresheet so that we know what *beresheet* means, because, as the Zohar tells us, knowledge is the connection. By having knowledge of this insight, and by retaining it, the Zohar discloses, we are connecting to the seed of Creation—the beginning. The start of any process is where everything is contained, and thus can be managed. However, once things begin to manifest, they can get out of hand.

Nothing can come out of the seed, the Keter. For a seed to grow into a tree, it must undergo a process. By having this kind of knowledge of Beresheet, we are implanted with a complete understanding of the universe. The reason we want to understand the universe at its very beginning is because this knowledge puts us in control—and not subject to the signs of the zodiac, the stars and planets. As human beings, we do not want to be governed by the cosmos—we want to have power over it.

The Zohar says that the reason *yir'at HaShem* is the first precept mentioned at the beginning of the Bible is because without this consciousness, we are subject to different chaotic conditions. And this was not the purpose of Creation nor the intent of the Creator. The Zohar says that by having *yir'at HaShem*, even if we cannot make things good for everyone, at least we can experience good for ourselves. *Beresheet* refers to achieving a level of consciousness where we control our reality.

Mount Sinai

The Zohar says that at the Revelation event on Mount Sinai, God came to all the nations of the world. This is because Revelation was not solely for the Israelites, it was for all people of the world.

Rabbi Shlomo Yitzchaki (1040-1105), also known by the acronym Rashi, a medieval rabbi and commentator on the Five Books of Moses and the Talmud, says that the biblical statement *Beresheet bara Elokim* was meant to provide all humanity with the power of revelation—certainty at the level of Keter, the seed level—so that we could understand and see how to become masters of our universe, and how we can adjust ourselves to access and tap into the energy of Israel, which is the energy center of the world.

At the Revelation on Mount Sinai, God had approached each nation to give them the ability and the possibility to access all that the Bible has to offer. However, according to the Zohar, the nations refused—they did not want the responsibility. From the Zohar we understand that it was not a matter of the Creator's preference, but rather it was a choice to accept such a great reward—the control of our own destiny, which came with a great responsibility.

Some interpret Revelation to mean that God revealed Himself. Does this imply that the people saw God? We do not understand the essence of God. What we can comprehend are the attributes of His energy, which the kabbalists refer to as Light. The Bible tells us that the Israelites at Mount Sinai "saw the Voice." How can one see a sound? According to the Zohar, "voice" is Zeir Anpin—a vibration. A vibration is beyond feeling—it exists on a manifested level.

Humanity is the initiator of all harmony in the world. If we are fragmented, then a fragmented vibration is spread into every area of this universe. If our actions are negative, this will be the vibration and manifestation that exists throughout the world. Therefore, all of Creation—the animal and vegetable kingdoms—is begging us to live in unity because all other kingdoms, besides that of humankind, do live in unity. Humankind controls every aspect of this universe. The purpose of the study of Kabbalah is to raise our level of consciousness so that we can improve both our physical and mental well-being.

The Zohar says:

> This is why it says Beresheet, about Chochmah, which is composed of *Bet Resheet*. The numerical value of *Bet* is two, because Chochmah is the second of the Ten Sefirot. It is

called *Resheet* (Beginning) because, although the Supernal and concealed Keter is the first of the Sefirot, Keter is not included in the number of the Sefirot. Thus, the second, namely Chochmah, is considered as the *Resheet* (Beginning). Therefore, it is considered *Bet Resheet*: *Bet*, since it is the second Sefira in the order of the emanation of the Sefirot, and "Beginning," since it is the first in the counting, as Keter is not counted. Furthermore, just as the Upper Chochmah is a beginning, so is the Lower Chochmah a beginning. From the Upper Chochmah down to Malchut, which is the Lower Chochmah, there is no Sefira that may receive for itself the illumination of Chochmah. Hence, *Bet* should not be separated from *Resheet*. In other words, this *Bet* alludes to Malchut, which is the Lower Chochmah. Since there is no other Sefira between them that may receive the illumination of Chochmah, Malchut and *Resheet* should be joined to form *Beresheet*.

—Zohar, Beresheet A 36:340

The Zohar explains that *Resheet chochmah yir'at HaShem* is a code. If we can connect to the "all-seeing," then we are "full of wisdom." The Gemara says, "The wise individual is he who sees all of the future manifestations." *Bet* represents both Chochmah and Binah—Chochmah is from the point of view of the Light, and Binah is from the point of view of the Vessel.

The Zohar says that Keter is never included because it is the seed. A seed is planted before it can develop into a tree. It must disappear as it is the indirect cause of the tree. What does the root do? It establishes only one tree. But the potential of that seed, like the sperm, has infinite possibilities. Therefore, Keter will always remain a concealed aspect. We cannot connect with it but we can connect to everything that emerges from it, beginning with the Sefira of

Chochmah. The Zohar explains that, when we can raise our level of consciousness, we rise above the process of trial and error.

The power of seeing is in Beresheet 1:1, whether we are conscious of it or not. Sometimes we are better off not being *conscious* of all of the details. In other words, we should *know* the details but, at the same time, we should make a connection to the higher level of consciousness—the one that sees from beginning to end. The purpose of connecting with this one verse is because it is the beginning of everything, meaning that tomorrow is included in today.

Heavens and Earth—Bringing Together Malchut and Binah

In the sentence, *Beresheet bara Elokim et haShamayim ve'et ha'Aretz,* the two words *et* and *ve'et* (*the* Heavens *and the* Earth) seem superfluous. The Bible could have simply said "Heavens and Earth." The Zohar says that both uses of the word *et* are a connection to the world of manifestation—our world. The Zohar further explains that in the beginning, God created the universe with *midat hadin* (the attribute of pure, strict judgment). In other words, cause is followed by immediate effect—stealing would result in the loss of a hand, and murder would result in death—God Forbid. But God saw that the world could not exist with only the attribute of harsh judgment. The world also needed *midat harachamim* (the attribute of mercy) because a world governed by the attribute of harsh judgment or immediate effect, does not leave room for free will. Who would steal or behave immorally if retribution was immediate? The word *rachamim*, in essence, means "compassion" or "mercy"—although this is not the complete implication of the word. It also refers to the concept of "time." If stealing was promptly followed by consequences or punishment, there could be no free will. The attribute of mercy and the aspect of time create the space for free will to correct our actions.

When we plant a seed, the ultimate manifestation we seek is not the trunk, branches or leaves—it is the ripened fruit. In the final analysis, Kabbalah teaches that life is all about fulfilling the true desire. We want our desires realized—but for most of us, the process is not what we seek. The process is the means to achieving the ultimate manifestation, called Malchut. Man is the personification of Malchut, Desire to Receive. The realm of Binah is the Desire to Share, which is something human beings are not born with. The Zohar reveals that, with the inclusion of *et* and *ve'et*, God merged Malchut with the consciousness of Binah or Understanding.

There are spiritual laws in place in the universe, and the Zohar explains that, at one time, there were also such laws in our physical human kingdom, but these laws would have removed the aspect of free will, and free will was necessary to give humanity space to awaken our own compassion. Thus, there was a merging of Malchut and Binah, and the Desire to Receive now took on an additional characteristic, one of sharing. God not only created the Heavens and Earth with their innate DNA characteristics, but also that, through the use of the *et* and *ve'et*, the attribute of mercy was created so as to provide a chance at free will. Had humanity been left solely with our own Desire to Receive, how could we have prevailed against that instinct and developed the Desire to Share?

The Sefira of Malchut (Desire to Receive) is the ultimate manifestation of everything. All members of the animal kingdom are not taught how to behave—they behave by instinct. Humankind, however, if not taught, could go through life and not know even how to reproduce. This is not an inborn system with us. An animal instinctively knows its mother, which is not so with humans. When an animal cares for its newborn, the care is inbuilt.

The opposite is true of a human mother and child—they have no concept of each other at all.

The animal kingdom lives within certain rules of the universe, and does not acquire additional knowledge. With human beings, knowledge is acquired, and is not instinctive. Some might say that an animal has a higher level of consciousness than a human being, since the animal's knowledge is inborn. However, we know this is not the case. For the animal, from birth to death, instinct has been programmed in its DNA. With a human being, everything is wide open, and there are no preprogrammed instincts. When a human being has a premonition, this is not an instinct—since instinct is programmed in the DNA, and only exists in non-human kingdoms of the universe. In the human kingdom it is entirely different because we have total free will.

Therefore, the Bible uses the words *et* and *ve'et*, indicating that there was *an addition* to Creation—humanity was given free will. But along with free will came a problem: When we do something wrong, we do not, of necessity, experience the effect of that action right away. Free will comes with the concept of time. If we thought that our wrongdoing would require immediate repayment, we would never endeavor to steal or murder or do any wrong to our fellow beings, or to the other kingdoms of Creation.

Everything that evolved from *Yom Echad* or "One Day" was already included within this day as one unified whole. Therefore, the Zohar says that in the Age of Aquarius—the time in which we now live—the universe will revert to that age of *midat hadin* (immediate effect). This is why Rav Shimon says, "Woe unto this generation and praiseworthy unto this generation," because this generation will see more than any generation since the time of the Revelation. At the time of the Revelation, everyone had true sight. So will it be in the Age of Aquarius. *Yir'ah* means seeing the whole picture, and this is more connected to din or "judgment."

The Zohar says that when we see the strings of the universe, we will no longer want to steal—not because *we* are going to be punished, not out of fear, but because we can see the immediate consequences of our actions. Our true seeing is not out of fear, since this world also has that aspect of *rachamim* or "mercy"—which means we have time. Even with this aspect of God-fearing, most people will still take a chance and steal when no one is around, especially if they are in a dire situation—perhaps their children have not eaten in days, for example.

How do we reconcile these two opposite factors of *din* or "judgment," (the state of immediate retribution), and *rachamim* or "mercy" (time)? If someone has *Yir'ah*, and can see how their actions fit into the whole scheme of things, knowing that whatever they are doing or want to do is against the strings of the universe and that, ultimately, they will pay the price, then this is *din*. This individual is not going to steal or murder because God is watching them, but rather they will avoid such acts because they see from beginning to end, and thus understand that they have to pay a price, which may not happen immediately because it could just as well happen a few years hence.

Fear or awe of God (*Yir'ah*) is not that we fear God *because* He will smite us if we perform negative actions. When the Bible stresses "Thou shall not steal" or "Thou shall not kill," this, by and of itself, will never be a deterrent for people. The Bible is explaining to us that we, and not the people around us, are affected by our negative activity. *Yir'ah* is the ability to see just how it affects us personally, and this is *midat hadin* (the attribute of pure, strict judgment).

Midat harachamim also has a price—and the price of delayed retribution is that we forget. With the aspect of mercy (time), retribution for our negative activity is not immediate and, as time goes by, we may even convince ourselves that what we did was for someone's benefit—or otherwise twist things to suit ourselves. As a result of this aspect of free will, a human being is able to operate on many different levels of understanding. One can justify anything, even murder. This is not done in the animal kingdom. The animal kingdom abides by strict rules.

2 The Earth was without form and empty, darkness was over the surface of the deep, and the Spirit of God hovered over the waters. 3 And God said, "Let there be light," and there was light. 4 And God saw the light that it was good, and God separated the light from the darkness. 5 God called the light "day," and the darkness God called "night." And there was evening, and there was morning—One Day.

Operating on Two Levels

If yesterday, tomorrow, and today are preordained, it would seem that there is no free will. This is why it is said that God created darkness, which gives us the freedom to choose between good and evil.

The Zohar says that Light is a force that never undergoes a change, yet there are many different manifestations of the Lightforce of God. For example, electricity itself does not undergo any change. The poles in a lightbulb manifest electricity as plus and minus and, just as an electric current undergoes change and becomes manifest when it is concealed, so it is with the Lightforce of God. The Lightforce takes on different forms and creates darkness, meaning that, once the Light becomes manifest, it operates as plus and minus—and for this there is a price. When we look at the picture of a landscape and focus in on only one beautiful tree, we lose sight of the rest of the picture. Once we zoom in, we limit our perception. This is the price.

Seeing the entire picture involves operating on two levels at the same time. We cannot operate on one and then jump to the other. We have to be conscious of everything around us and, at the same time, be conscious of the specific. We want to be able to connect to the beginning and the end, along with everything else involved.

We have to deal with each day, even though there is a bigger picture we may not see—and if we do not deal with each day, then it will only remain in potential. We cannot become spiritual people by not being involved with anything of a physical nature. Spirituality is getting involved, and then distancing ourselves, knowing there is a price, and how that price is going to affect us. It is important that we stay cognizant of the price at all times, not only in the moment but also knowing that if nothing happens in the immediate present, there is also a tomorrow.

Real Beginnings

The Zohar says that, if we do not know the beginning, the root of things, we cannot really have clarity. It is only when we inspect the seed that we know what kind of tree will grow. DNA reveals everything that is going to happen—why one person is predisposed to an illness and another is not. Inspecting and exploring the root of things is essential to understanding not only ourselves but everything else as well because no branch can be different to that which the seed itself dictates.

There are two volumes of explanation in the Zohar on the portion of Beresheet concerning Creation—how this world came into existence, and what happened afterwards. According to the Bible, and our Kabbalistic Calendar, this year is 5757 (1997). There is a difference of opinion between religion and science about the origin of the universe. According to quantum theory, there are different levels or frames of reference, meaning relativity—I see something one way and another person sees it another way. All are right because within every frame of reference there are many different dimensions.

The Zohar explains that Beresheet One refers to the Infinite Dimension, where there is no physical measurement. It is not discussing day and night but rather concepts of thought beyond time, space, and motion.

With thought, we can travel the entire Earth. We can picture, in our mind, each city we visit along the way in a matter of seconds. To physically experience this trip would require weeks, months or more, but for the mind there is another frame of reference. When the Bible speaks of "days," it does not mean days as in 24 hours, it is discussing time in another framework.

We turn to the Zohar for an explanation—and we always read or scan the Aramaic. Just listening to these words immediately opens up another dimension in our mental computer. When we scan the Zohar, even without understanding a word of it, the mere contact with its Aramaic words connects with the entire dimension that a particular word is describing. The same is true when we meditate on the letters of the Hebrew alphabet because it is through the letters of the Hebrew alphabet that everything came into existence. They created the world.

Binding by Striking

The Zohar, in Beresheet A 1:1, says:

> With the beginning of the manifestation of the King's will, that is, when the King desired to emanate and create the world, a hard spark made an engraving upon the Supernal Light. This hard spark, which emanated from the most

concealed of all concealed things, from the secret of the Endless Light, took a shapeless form. The spark was then inserted into the center of a circle that was neither white nor black nor red nor green, nor any color at all. When it began its measurements, it created colors that shone into the empty space and the engraving. From within the spark—this hard spark—a fountain spouted, from which the shades down Below received their colors.

Here Rav Shimon is speaking about the concept of Binding by Striking. When we strike something, we connect with it—which seems to be a paradox. Normally we understand striking as pushing away but what we discover from the Zohar, is that by striking we actually draw toward ourselves. The Zohar says that from Binding by Striking comes the secret of the *Ein Sof* or Endless Light—the ultimate reality that exists beyond time, space, and motion. We see from the passage above that, in the Endless Light, the four essential colors—white, red, black or green—do not exist. There was no variation of color because in the *Ein Sof* there are no degrees of different intelligence—there is only one thought. The *Ein Sof* was one unified whole. In the beginning, there was only a Desire to Share. Only after the Endless Light did things become differentiated, able to be measured by development and manifestation in different frames of reference, different intelligences, and different thoughts.

In his commentary on the Zohar, Rav Ashlag (1885-1954), says that *beresheet* means *bara sheet*. In Aramaic, *bara* means "created" and *sheet* is "six." Hence: "He created six." The word "six" is a code for *Shamayim* or "Heavens," the intelligence of Desire to Share, and *ha'Aretz* or "Earth," which is a code for Malchut, is the thought energy-intelligence of Desire to Receive. "Six" is the aspect of sharing, and Malchut is the recipient of everything, indicating that everything on Earth receives from the cosmos, in one way or another.

To help us understand this even further, Rav Ashlag explains Binding by Striking by comparing the concept to someone striking a rock with another rock and creating a spark. Why does a spark result when we strike two stones together?

The Zohar says everything that ultimately becomes revealed does so because there is a Force, the Light, that wants to become revealed—and that this Light is infinite. From a kabbalistic point of view, there is Light even in a dark room. One way this Lightforce becomes revealed is through an electric lightbulb. The bulb does not create light; all it does is reveal that which is already there—the light that was concealed before.

King Solomon said there is nothing new under the sun. Everything that becomes manifest already exists before it is revealed. Thought is Light; it is energy that wants to become revealed but must first be revealed in the mind. From there it can then become manifest on a physical level.

Even when we try to sit quietly, we are bombarded with thoughts that want to be expressed. We cannot stop thoughts from penetrating our consciousness. When we think, we are, in effect, revealing thoughts that have come to our mind—and the specific thoughts that come to one person do not come to someone else.

We can also transfer our thought energy-intelligence to another person or thing. Thought is so powerful that we can influence people, and we can make them do what we want them to do. If someone has a strong nature, they can influence those who have weaker temperaments. One does not necessarily have to use physical strength to influence others.

God's sharing is the Light of *Ein Sof*, which encompasses every force that exists in this world. It is anything that wants to move from one place outward into another. Whether my hand strikes a rock, or I want to influence someone, this is the same Force of *Ein Sof*. The thought energy-intelligence wants to expand. When someone has an idea, and they want everyone to believe in the idea, he expands and tries to exert an influence over other people. When a number of people accept this idea, there has been a manifestation, an extension of his thought into others.

When we throw a rock into water, the water cannot push the rock back because the rock is more powerful. If we throw it down with a force, this means we are more powerful than both the rock and the water. I can push my hand right into water because water does not have the capacity to resist my energy. However, it is not so easy to penetrate a table. In other words, there is a thought energy-intelligence called "table" that has an energy-intelligence, which can resist my force. We are not speaking about physical force here, we are discussing the force of atoms. There are infinite atoms in the air, and we can run our hands through them, but we cannot go through the table because there is an energy-intelligence that can resist us.

When I hit a rock with another rock, a spark comes out because the rock is resisting the penetration of my force. A spark comes out of this resistance. Every time there is a clash, there is a spark, and sometimes we see the spark, sometimes we do not. When two entities meet and one resists the other, like in a lightbulb, a spark emerges. This spark is revealing light that is already there. What is revealed by this spark is a circuit of energy between these two people. For there to be a circuit of energy—meaning a continuous flow, and not a short-circuit—there must be some form of resistance. This is a filament. When resistance is functional, we have a circuit. Without a filament, the bulb will not light up, despite the fact that electricity has come into it.

Does this mean that to create a circuit of energy, we should resist or oppose another's opinion? No, resistance does not mean "I don't want to listen." Rather it means that when we listen sincerely and engage in questions to better understand, the questioning is really the resistance. Someone who only wants to tell others but has no time for resistance in the form of questions or feedback, will not be remembered well by others. Such a person did not create an impact because, to create a resistance, a spark, there has to be an exchange of positions. In other words, first there is a sharing of an idea, and then there is becoming a listener, the receiver of another's idea. When each becomes both the sharer and the receiver, there is a circuit of energy. But if the energy flows only one way, there is no possible contact. Contact happens by resistance, which ultimately creates a greater and greater exchange of ideas. Resistance creates a circuit of energy—nothing more and nothing less. This is Binding by Striking.

The Zohar's explanation of Beresheet 1:1 describes an occurrence that sounds much like a description of the Big Bang. At the time of Creation, because of the concept of Bread of Shame, the receiver or the Vessel, resisted the Desire to Share of the Creator, since it did not want to receive God's beneficence without earning it—thus creating Binding by Striking. At that moment, a spark (the Big Bang) erupted because there was a conflict: God wanted to share, and because the Vessel resisted, there was no longer an exchange between the Vessel and the Creator.

In his commentary on the Zohar, Rav Ashlag says that what sparked the Creation was *Bara Sheet*—Binah consciousness created Six and One. The Six thought energy-intelligences known as Zeir Anpin—Chesed, Gevurah, Tiferet, Netzach, Hod, Yesod—are all aspects of the Lightforce of God, and are what make movement. The One or Malchut, is a revealment of the Lightforce of God.

The first confrontation was between the Six (*Shamayim* or "Heavens")—*Zeir Anpin*, the six different aspects of the Lightforce—and the One (*Aretz* or "Earth"), which is Malchut. Because the Lightforce is sharing, and Malchut is receiving, they are two opposites in conflict, and thus produced a spark. This spark first emanated, not as a day, but as, "There is evening, there is morning, *Yom Echad* (One Day)."

The Zohar raises the question of why the Bible says *Yom Echad* (One Day), and not *Yom Rishon*, (First Day). The Zohar then answers that the word *echad* indicates "one" or "unified," and the word *yom* means a thought energy-intelligence (or a Sefira), and not something physical. By clashing, the Heavens and the Earth complement each other. The sharer becomes the receiver, and the receiver becomes the sharer. Restriction came into effect in that first moment of Creation, and there was unity because each became interchangeable with the other. This is why the Bible says *Yom Echad* and not *Yom Rishon*.

The Zohar explains that *Yom Echad* is a thought energy-intelligence of Chesed—it is unified, inclusive of everything—but it is only in potential. A seed is one unified whole—the trunk, leaves, and fruit are all there in potential. According to the secret of Beresheet, when we plant a seed in the ground, there is an immediate clash. The earth covers the seed and conceals it, which is the opposite of the seed's innate nature or desire. What is the desire of the seed? It is to become manifested, to be revealed as a tree. Because of gravity, we may think the earth draws everything to itself. However, while the earth has the capacity to draw, it also has an inbuilt capacity to resist. When the seed is planted, the earth draws it in, and also resists what the seed wants. There is a clash between the two. The seed wants to become revealed, the earth conceals it.

This is the secret of the *Tzimtzum*—which is what scientists call the Big Bang. But the Zohar says that this is an ongoing process in our lives. Each time we restrict, we recreate *Tzimtzum*. By not conforming, not agreeing we can have circuits of energy—but there must be an aspect of resistance. This resistance does not affect the life-giving force because the same Lightforce of God that is in me is in everyone else.

The word *echad* indicates that all diversified factors are merged into one unified unit. Once the seed becomes manifest, it is no longer a unified whole. The trunk emerges, and the trunk does not have a root or the fruit—division has occurred. But, in its original state, a seed is one unified whole.

The Zohar also says that the word *vayikra*, in Beresheet 1:5, is a code. Here the word *vayikra* means "to invite, tap or draw," rather than its literal translation, which is "to call"—*vayikra* in this particular verse indicates the different levels of consciousness that were drawn down into this universe on the days of Creation. This is the Sefirot of Chesed, Gevurah, and Tiferet, which are already included in *Yom Echad*. Although these three Sefirot are unique levels of consciousness, they are unified on the first day of Creation, and are known as the Upper Triad of the *Magen David* (Shield of David). The Lower Triad is made up of the three levels of consciousness known as Netzach, Hod, and Yesod. The creation of the *Magen David*, the Shield of David, is what Beresheet One is all about.

The Upper Triad is the level of potential energy, and the Lower Triad is the level of actual energy. Let us examine the process of manifestation as it happens in this physical world. Before the creation of something, first there is a flash of an idea—the potential—which must contain all three sources of energy, Right (Chesed), Left (Gevurah), and Central (Tiferet). It is not a complete idea unless it contains all of these three characteristics. For example, when there is an idea to build an apartment complex, the first thing we do is perceive the design mentally. This is the Upper Triad—the potential. Next, we ask an architect to design the details of our vision, which is the Lower Triad—the actual. This simple procedure is something we accept as a natural process—but from whence does it come? It all originates right here in the Creation. Day One of Beresheet One is the creation of all manner of things we take for granted, things that had to first exist in a potential state, and only then become manifest by us.

The Zohar explains that *yom* or "day" is Right Column, and *laila* or "night" is Left Column, in the Lower Triad—where it becomes manifest. Both are still in a metaphysical state—they are still an intangible thought. But there are two levels. One is the idea, and the other is how to manifest this idea. All six Sefirot ultimately became manifested as one unified concept—*laila*, which is the seventh Sefira.

There are those who have great ideas and yet they lose money, and there are others who have the same idea and yet make money. Why? It is because while the idea may have been just as great for the one who lost money, the idea was not thought out properly in his mind before he set it down on paper. When everything in the mind is as one unified unit, there is no need to worry about how it becomes manifest. If things are clear in the mind, they manifest properly. The only time ideas are not manifested properly or turn out to be disastrous, is when they are not unified in the mind. Day One of Creation concerns all of the energies becoming unified.

When we look at the physical world—which has the most influence upon us—we see everything as fragmented, separated from each other. Thus the conclusions we reach or the solutions we apply to problems are not necessarily sound, and thus may result in distortions of what was intended. When we have a complete picture of all the aspects, it is *Echad*—and then everything we do will be unified, not fragmented.

Names of God as Levels of Consciousness

God has many Names, which are all different levels of consciousness. When we are discussing Binah, Briah or Bara, we are speaking of another level of consciousness called "God." When we are discussing the Tetragrammaton—*Yud, Hei, Vav,* and *Hei*—this is another level of consciousness, of thought energy-intelligence. *Elokim* means a lower level of consciousness, and already deals with our world. This verse alone is dealing with the creation of different energy levels—the how, what, and when.

Shamayim or "Heavens" is called Six because in the Heavens there are the six major Heavenly bodies—Sun, Mercury, Mars, Jupiter, Uranus, and Saturn—which represent the astral influence of sharing. All astral influences are funneled through the Six, and this bundle is delivered to us by the moon. Malchut or Earth is the revealment of these Six.

The Bible says *Yom Echad* because at the beginning, in Sefira Chesed, there is a clash that creates unity. If two opposites do not communicate with each other there can never be unity; if they never talk, they will never get together. When each expresses their self in agreement or as opposite to the other, this is the beginning of a possible unification or joining of the two. But, if they do not meet, even in clash, they will never be unified.

The Nature of Yom Echad (One Day)

The Zohar says that everything was formed on Day One of Creation, and that throughout the following six days, the acts of Creation continued. It explains further that the reason the Bible says *Yom Echad* (One Day) is because on Day One, everything in Creation existed in seed form—and will exist in that way forever. After Day One of Creation, there came the sin of Adam, which brought disunity.

Beresheet 1:5 says that when God separated the Light from the darkness, "He called the Light day and the darkness He called night, and there was evening and there was morning—One Day." But if the Sun and the Moon were only created on the Fourth Day, how did day and night occur on the first day?

Both the Zohar and the Talmud say that everything in the physical world is illusory. The Bible knew that it would take time for humankind to accept this concept. The meaning of *Yom Echad* or One Day is that there will come a time when people will have *Mashiach* (Messiah) Consciousness, and will comprehend that there is no time, space or motion.

Time, space, and motion still weigh heavily on our daily lives because we cannot grasp the idea that they are an illusion. Shabbat is an illusion but we observe it because we live with a physical consciousness. The Zohar and the Talmud say that when we reach *Mashiach* Consciousness, we will transcend this physical illusion—but until then we have to use these tools.

The Bible tells us that the true reality is an energy consciousness we cannot grasp or measure with the five senses. This energy influences us to the positive or the negative. Although we are subject to this influence, when we understand its nature, we can learn how to make use of it. The negative exists alongside the positive, and we must deal with both forces.

The true reality is an energy of understanding, not the physical world. Chaos is a lack of understanding. On Shabbat morning, we tap into the energy that can assist us to achieve dominion over the physical dimension. We come to The Kabbalah Centres to capture this unique energy, which teaches us that the physical reality is not the root of chaos.

In the portion of Beresheet, we are told that the immaterial aspect of reality is a development—an evolution of our consciousness. We are talking about Sefirot, energy, Names of Divine Inspiration. *Yom Echad* or One Day of Creation is about the energy-intelligence of Chesed, which in the physical reality is water. The Zohar explains that Chesed is also the power of *echad* or "one," which is unity. To this day, it is a fundamental truth that the world cannot exist without water.

The Flawless Universe and Chaos

How can we comprehend billions of years, when we have only been incarnating on this Earth for less than six thousand years? All views of Creation are inherently riddled with contradictions, but the Zohar's vision is so far advanced, that it represents matters about which science can only speculate. The 99 percent of our being, the immaterial part, which we know as reality, is not what the Bible is talking about with relation to the first seven days of Creation. We are not discussing the 99 Percent Reality—which also includes the potential for chaos—but rather what the Bible is talking about is the ultimate reality that we all aspire to connect with, and this is called *Etz HaChayim* or Tree of Life Reality. In this reality, the chaos that humankind has experienced since the fall of Adam cannot enter. This portion teaches us that whatever will emerge in the future is already incorporated in the first seven days of Creation—in potential form. When we listen to the Torah reading on Shabbat Beresheet, we connect to the time before blockages caused untoward things to happen in our lives.

The Zohar explains that everything in Creation was present from the beginning in a potential, perfect form, and that just because we cannot see this potential, it does not mean we can deny its existence. The kabbalists were always aware of realms that exist beyond this physical reality—the Tree of Life Reality and the Tree of Knowledge Reality. At the very beginning, there was the Flawless Universe but there also existed the possibility of humankind's intervention to create chaos. Although it defies understanding, the potential for chaos is ever-present but something has to activate this potential. Leave a seed on a table for a million years and what will happen? Nothing. What is required is intervention—for a tree to grow, someone must take that seed from the table and plant it in rich soil.

Unfortunately today, we see more of chaos than we do of the Flawless Universe known as the Tree of Life Reality. Beresheet is the most important Bible portion because it is the beginning of life before humankind's intervention—before Adam and Eve and the temptation of the snake, which disrupted the Flawless Universe. With this portion we have the opportunity to connect to the moment when separation did not exist. We are discussing creating a protection shield that can bring us into the realm of the Flawless Universe. For the first time in civilization, we are attempting to intervene in the progress of chaos by bringing back human potential. We can travel back in time and prevent disasters, even if we do not understand the process. You do not have to accept it—we, at the Centres, are merely sharing knowledge.

Inconsistencies and the Zohar

The first verse says "He created the Heavens and the Earth." We understand that it could not mean Heaven and Earth as we know them because it was not until the third day that Heaven and Earth were created. Then God says "let there be light," and He sees that the Light is good. What is this Light? Is this when God created our sun, the major light in our sky? No. That was created on the fourth day. Then darkness appears. God had not yet created the sun or moon, so where did the darkness come from? Then, all of a sudden, water appears. Where did the water come from? It does not even say that God created it. Nowhere in this is water mentioned.

There are many commentaries on Day One of Creation, and all of them—even that of Rashi (Rabbi Shlomo Itzchaki)—are totally incomprehensible. We are fortunate with the Zohar that it is all explained so simply.

6 And God said, "Let there be a firmament between the waters to divide water from water." 7 So God made the firmament and divided the water under the firmament from the water above the firmament. And it was so. 8 God called the firmament "heaven." And there was evening, and there was morning—Second Day.

Water and the Energy of Chesed

On the Second Day, God separated the water and the dry land. There is no mention of water on Day One of Creation. From whence came this water that God separated into Upper and Lower Waters? On the Second Day, when there are two—meaning more than one—there is no longer a unified whole. Now there are two distinct elements: Upper Water and Lower Water.

Regarding the Second Day of Creation, in Beresheet 1:6-8, the Zohar says it refers to how negativity became manifest. Although negativity was created on Day One of Creation, it was still in complete unity with the positive aspect, and did not desire to cancel out the Right Column, the energy of Chesed.

When God made a separation between the Upper and the Lower Waters on the Second Day, this brought about stage two of Creation—the manifestation of the Left Column. This fragmentation was necessary, otherwise everything would remain in a potential form as one unified whole. Water is the internal energy force of Chesed (Loving Kindness). Chesed is a unified state—and thus water means a unified state. The division in the waters on Day Two concerns the unified Sefira of Chesed becoming fragmented.

When we plant a seed in the ground, a force separates the seed from the root, and then again the force separates the stem from the root, and so on. What is this force that makes the root emerge as a separate unit? The force that can change the composition of something is known as Left Column energy.

The Zohar says:

> "And God said, 'Let there be a firmament in the midst of the waters.'" (Beresheet 1:6) This phrase alludes to a detailed reform of the separation of the Upper from the Lower Waters according to the secret of the Left. Here, the dispute according to the secret of the Left occurred. Until this point, referring to the first day, reference is made to the Right. But on the second day, reference is to the secret of the governing of the Left. Because of this, a great dispute broke out on the second day between the two sides. The Left wanted to cancel the governing power of the Right entirely, while the Right wanted to cancel the governing power of the Left entirely. The Right, which is the secret of Chesed and the first day, is the perfection of all. Because of this, everything was written in the Right on the first day. This means that all the seven days, which are the seven Sefirot, emerged in it and are hinted in it because every perfection depends on the Right side. When the rule of the Left was aroused, its dispute with the Right began and the fire of anger in that dispute became fierce. From this dispute, *Gehenom* was created. So *Gehenom* was awakened, and created by the Left, and cleaved to it, which means that whoever wants to strengthen the Left shall fall into *Gehenom*, which originates from it.
> —Zohar, Beresheet A 6:44

What a revelation this is! We have heard the expression that, if we are bad, we will end up in *Gehenom* (Hell). Here, the Zohar makes it very clear that Hell was never created by God. Hell emerged from a dispute between the Right and the Left. In other words, we create our own Hell on Earth.

Where there is one force, the other one has to appear. The world of fragmentation must exist. Yet, it does not have to exist in a fiery or angry manner. We can always sit down and say, "Please enlighten me. Maybe you know something I don't know." As children, most of us are taught that God created the Garden of Eden for the righteous, and Hell to punish the evil—but this is not so. We do not have to wait until we pass away to experience Heaven or Hell—we experience both of them on this Earth right now.

The Zohar continues:

> In his wisdom, Moses looked into this and learned about the work of Creation. In the work of Creation, there was a dispute between the Left and the Right. And in that dispute, which the Left provoked, *Gehenom* was created, and *Gehenom* held onto the Left. The central pillar, which is Tiferet, entered between them on the third day, ending the dispute and bringing the two sides to an agreement. So *Gehenom* removed itself from the Left and descended Below. The Left joined the Right, and there was peace everywhere.
> —Zohar, Beresheet A 6:45

From the Zohar we understand that the energy of *machloket* or "quarrel" originated in Day Two of Creation. We also learn how the energy of separation becomes manifest, and that it need not govern us.

Moses dwelled upon the first three days of Creation in Beresheet, and he discovered the secret of how to bring two opposites into a unified whole. The Zohar says that only by fully understanding the implications of Day Two could Moses settle any dispute between two individuals. In other words, whether in a family, business or friendship, it is very rare to find two people who think exactly alike, and have no diverse opinions—indeed it is so rare that it almost does not exist.

On Day Two there was a separation in the waters—they did not want to merge. So God created a *rakia* or "firmament," meaning a separation. The Bible uses the Hebrew word *mavdil* to describe this separation of the waters from each other. The word *havdalah* is derived from the word *mavdil*. When we perform the practice of *Havdalah* at the conclusion of Shabbat, there is a misconception that what we are doing is establishing a separation between the Holy (Shabbat) and the mundane (the other six days of the week). The Zohar, however, says that the word *havdalah* means "fulcrum" or "synthesizing." By performing the Havdalah we are not creating separation, rather we are merging the Shabbat—which is Holy and represents abundance and all things good—with the mundane, which does not have the qualities of Shabbat, and thus making them both coexist as one unified whole.

The light in a lightbulb cannot appear without the separation between positive and negative poles. This is the way light is revealed in the physical world. Separation does not mean complete disconnection. *Mavdil* means a separation that brings about a connection—the joining of forces. For two to become one, first there must be separation.

Moses understood that having a Left and a Right did not mean these two opposites could not merge. Diversity of opinion is not a bad thing—quite the contrary. However, what is necessary is restriction.

God created the Firmament because separation would have to exist in this world. Separation is Central Column—a force present in this world even when diversity exists. This is what Binding by Striking means. When we perform *Havdalah*, what we are doing is creating a restriction against the energy of Shabbat, so that it can spring back into the rest of the week, causing the Light of Shabbat to merge with the weekdays, and the weekdays to become one with Shabbat.

Firming Up the Firmament

Day Two of Creation speaks about a Firmament (Heaven) that divides the waters. What does this mean? Why was it necessary to divide the waters on Day Two? What was wrong with the first day? And if God has already created Heaven and Earth on the first day, why is the Firmament also given the name "Heaven"? What is this section talking about? The Zohar says that when God created the force of restriction by creating the Firmament, God called the *Rakia* (Firmament), *Shamayim* (Heaven). The word *Shamayim* is made up of two words—*esh* (fire) and *mayim* (water)—thus Heaven is made of fire and water. Elsewhere in the Bible we find this:

> A similar dispute occurred between Korach and Aaron, the Left against the Right. Moses tried his best to reconcile them, but the Left did not want to be reconciled. So Korach became stronger and overcame Aaron... Korach did not wish to be attached Above, namely to the structure of Holiness, and join the Right, like the Left on high... Because of this, Korach did not want Moses to settle this dispute, since it was not for Heaven's sake (with pure

intentions). He had no respect for the Celestial Glory, which is the *Shechinah*, and refused to acknowledge the work of Creation. This means that he denied the settlement of the Central Column in the work of Creation. He wanted only the Left to govern... Therefore, Korach cleaved on to what he deserved; he reached *Gehenom*, as written, "They went down alive into Sheol."
—Numbers 16:33

In this situation with Korach, the Zohar says that Moses understood why there could be people who are so divergent in their views. Korach was also from the tribe of Levi, like Moses and Aaron, and he accused Moses of nepotism, saying Moses was the ruler, and his brother Aaron was named High Priest—everything was becoming quite a family affair. Korach said that he wanted to be the High Priest. The whole story can be found in Numbers Chapter 16—and it ends with Korach being swallowed up by the earth.

With Aaron and Korach, Moses believed he knew how to be the synthesizer of these two individuals, and so he made an attempt to mediate between them. But the Left Column did not want conciliation. Korach did not want to rise above his natural inclination and become unified with the Right Column—as it is in Chesed. So Korach went down to *Gehenom*. The Zohar says that what occurred with Aaron and Korach helps us understand what happened on Day Two of Creation. Moses knew that there was no chance for him to mediate because Korach would not move from his place. Korach did not want to restrict at all—and so he was swallowed up.

Darkness is Mercy

From the Zohar, we understand that Beresheet 1:1 deals with
tikkunim or "spiritual corrections," and how we can improve
our physical and mental well-being. The Bible in general, and
Beresheet in particular, was not made available to us just to provide
information on how things began. We are meant to study it because
is important for us to comprehend the workings of the universe
and how we are connected to the entire cosmos. For this reason, I
feel it is vital to discuss the process up until the conclusion of the
Second Day of Creation. Beresheet is not about the creation of
days. So what did God create on these days? The Bible is unclear.
For example, Beresheet 1:1 says, "In the beginning, God created
the Heavens and the Earth." Then, in Beresheet 1:2, the Bible says,
"the Earth was unformed and void, and darkness was upon the face
of the deep, and the spirit of the Lord hovered over the face of the
waters." What are we being told here? If God has already created
Heaven and Earth, how then, in its completion, can the Earth
be *tohu vavohu*, a "vast wasteland," unformed and void? Another
question we can raise is did God create darkness? All that has been
written thus far is that God created Heaven and Earth—so where
did the darkness come from? And when the Bible says that God
hovered over the face of the waters, what waters were these? Does it
mean that there were waters already within the creation of Heaven
and Earth?

In Beresheet 1:3 it is written, "God said, 'Let there be light,' and
there was light and God saw that the light was good." Is the Bible
telling us that God created Heaven and Earth without light? In
other words, is Beresheet 1:2 complete? Is the light referred to
in Beresheet 1:3 emanating from the sun? If so, the sun was only
created on the Fourth Day.

Then Beresheet 1:4 says "…and God saw that it was good." Did God think He might have created something bad? What does the Bible mean when it says that God separated light from darkness? What could it have been like to have both light and darkness together? If you have light, then you no longer have darkness, and if you have darkness there is no light. Beresheet 1:5 tells us God called the light, "day," and the darkness He called "night." Why does God give another name to what was already there? Is it called "light" or "day"? And what does "day" mean? Does it mean daytime, and then does "darkness" mean nighttime? To make matters even more confusing, the verse then tell us that after light and darkness, day and night, there was evening, and there was morning. Are they really different?

For answers to these questions, we turn to the Zohar. By studying the Zohar we are not just acquiring wisdom, we also expand our consciousness.

There is nothing simple about Beresheet. Rav Shimon Bar Yochai, the author of the Zohar, says that the *p'shat* (the simple literal meaning of the Bible) is the most difficult aspect to understand. The word *p'shat* comes from the word *lehitpashet*, meaning "to undress." When we undress all of the layers, we arrive at the naked truth. When things are completely revealed and unveiled, this is a very high level of knowledge—one that few can achieve.

The Zohar addresses four crucial, coded words—*tohu, vohu, choshech*, and *Ruach*—explaining that the word *tohu* is a code for "restriction." Rav Shimon, Rav Isaac Luria (the Ari, 1534-1572), and other kabbalists explain that restriction, which removes Bread of Shame, is why we are here in this world. There are two restrictions, and the word *tohu* addresses itself to the First Restriction, which deals with *midat hadin* or "the aspect of strict judgment," immediate retribution, cause and effect without the aspect of time or mercy to buffer them.

And the word *vohu* is a code for the concept of *masach* or "curtain," which is the Second Restriction, known as *midat harachamim* or "the aspect of mercy"—a process involving compassion, meaning time. For instance, if a person stole something, their hand would not immediately fall off. Mercy does not mean there is no retribution for our negative activity. It means that that there is time to correct the negativity that we created.

To help us understand the concept of *masach*, consider a curtain in front of an open window. It can both block out the sunlight to some extent, and also break the movement of air. When the wind blows, the curtain will move back and forth. Although the *masach* is a form of restriction, it also moves with the wind—like free will. Every situation where a decision is required, and there is a back and forth movement, is called the curtain—*masach*.

In the two words, *tohu vavohu*, we learn the purpose of our being. We are here because of Bread of Shame. God has one thing in mind—to share His beneficence. This never changes. When things seem to go out of whack and are not in a stable order of sequence, it is because, in a previous lifetime, we upset this balance—and now we can ask God to help us out. We have all returned here to correct any injustice that was done in a prior lifetime, and we want to correct this because we want to be full of beneficence.

Tohu vevohu has nothing to do with a wasteland as we understand it. We can assume that, here, "wasteland" means a place where things do not come to fruition, where there is no beneficence. The Bible does not mean God created a wasteland but rather that the Vessels, we ourselves, created a condition whereby *we* can achieve our *tikkun*, and thus correct the purpose of our existence.

One of the questions we asked earlier was about where does the darkness come from. Rav Shimon says that darkness is dealing with what is known in kabbalistic terminology as *Tzimtzum Bet*, the Second Restriction that resulted in what we refer to as *midat harachamim* or "the aspect of mercy."

Choshech or "darkness" refers to the illusion of time, space, and motion, which is the structure of *midat harachamin*, where time and space give us the opportunity to correct things. Wherever there is darkness, it means a restriction of Light. When a person is in darkness—suffering from illness, hunger, poverty, and they need assistance—at such a time they are not filled with beneficence.

All the secrets of *tikkun*, and how to become the masters of our own destiny, are in Beresheet 1:1. There is an order and structure in this universe, and we are paying now for things we have done in a previous lifetime. The first verse reveals all the knowledge that permits us to get out of this lack of Light.

The Bible says, "The spirit (*Ruach*) of the Lord hovered over the face of the waters," What does *Ruach* mean? The Zohar explains that *Ruach* is *Tiferet*, the aspect of correction or the curtain, where we make decisions of free will to do something or not to do it. Darkness represents a lack, and *Ruach* represents the ability to correct that lack.

Tohu vavohu is discussing the First Restriction or *Tzimtzum Alef*—the aspect of harsh judgment. *Choshech* and *Ruach* deal with the Second Restriction or *Tzimtzum Bet*, where compassion entered, where *midat hadin* would not dictate matters—and a person now has the opportunity of free will to steal or not, and also to correct any misdeeds. In *Tzimtzum Alef*, in the first structure, if someone stole, their hand fell off. In the second aspect, they have the curtain, represented by *Ruach*. It appears as if the Lord has compassion for us because He structured the world so that, when we act negatively, we are permitted the opportunity to correct it. Therefore, compassion merely means we are given a little time to amend, to correct that which we have previously done.

The totality of Creation is what is being mentioned here. The Zohar tells us that all the secrets of knowledge that will permit us to get out of our dilemmas, out of this lack of Light, are in the first verse of Beresheet. It tells us that there is a structure, a law and order in the universe. Beresheet 1:1 tells us what we are doing here, and Beresheet 1:2 provides us with the structure of the universe.

Light is the term kabbalists use to refer to an intrinsic characteristic known as the Desire to Share. Light was always in existence, and darkness was created to permit us free will because, if we keep on receiving Light without earning it, we have Bread of Shame. God did not create darkness. The Vessel, which is us, asked the Light to stop Its beneficence because we felt Bread of Shame—in other words, we did not earn this Light, and we wanted a chance to do so. This is what *choshech* means.

God preceded everything. The positive-source energy always precedes negative energy—cause always precedes effect. Both the Talmud and the Zohar state that healing comes before the ailment. The solution is present before the problem begins, just as the antidote for poison ivy grows right next it. On the first day of Creation, God brought two different aspects together, although they were the same thing. It is like in the lightbulb, where we have a positive and a negative element that, together with a filament, produce Light.

When God said "Let there be light," this does not contradict what we have just discussed. The Lightforce of God has always existed. The Zohar says that on the First Day of Creation, there was Light—the positive and negative emerged as one unified whole, neither wanted to cancel out the other. This is why the Bible says, *vayehi erev vayehi boker yom Echad*, "there was evening there was morning, One Day," and it does not say, *vayehi erev vayehi boker, yom Rishon* (First Day). The Hebrew word *echad* means "unity."

"God saw that it was good," because the negative aspect participated in this unified action. If you have one pole without the other, you will not have circuitry. When there is the *Masach*, "curtain or filament," mentioned in Beresheet 1:2 with the words *Ruach* and *vevohu* or "to push back, restrict," then there is Light. What is our lesson here?

We learn that, even in a disagreement, where there are two opposing points of view, these can emerge either as a quarrel that brings infinite disparity or else it can bring a unified action. The Gemara says, "Every disagreement that is for a Heavenly purpose will have eternity." What does a Heavenly purpose mean? It means that, although there are opposing viewpoints, they can nevertheless produce mutual understanding. In other words, every disagreement does not have to lead to a separation; it could instead bring people together. Day One is teaching us that every disagreement can be another step in producing a unified action.

A disagreement, meaning yes and no, is not evil. On the contrary, yes and no is necessary to bring about unification. However, according to the Gemara, if the disagreement is not for the act of unification, then the plus and minus will remain eternally separated. Two seemingly different opinions can merge together as a unified whole and bring mutual understanding. If there is just one opinion without the other, there is no unification. There must be two opposites involved in any circuit of energy.

The greater the opposites, the more power they generate together. The 24,000 scholars of Rav Akiva perished because they disrespected each other. How could this be the case with such highly elevated souls? They were not perfect; if they were perfect, they would not be on this earthly plane. So we can understand that there was still something for them to correct. Because of their expanded consciousness, the evil inclination was that much greater. Without a greater evil inclination, where would the balance be? Where would free will be? The work of restriction never disappears. The Gemara is beautiful, showing us that, at any level, both a positive and a negative are essential. "And God saw that the light was good" indicates that there is a Central Column balancing positive and negative forces so that they are in harmony, rather than against each other.

Beresheet 1:4 says that God separated the light from the darkness. The Zohar says all the difficulties in the world emerged from the first day of Creation because the positive (Right) and negative (Left) aspects functioned as separate units. Each had a specific role and was not permitted to cancel out the other. The only way to have unification is when one aspect does not cancel out the other.

Second Day of Creation and the Energy of Water

The essence of One Day is the Sefira of Chesed, the first of the Seven Sefirot—Chesed, Gevurah, Tiferet, Netzach, Hod and Yesod. Chesed is the only component that can create unity beyond time, space, and motion. The physical manifestation of Chesed is water, which is also different from any other component of this universe. The Bible tells us that on the Second Day of Creation, there was a separation in the water—it was divided into Upper and Lower Waters.

We learn from the Ari that this first section of Beresheet is not referring to water as we know it. The water with which we are familiar came into existence in Beresheet Two, when all the other elements of physicality came into being. Beresheet One concerns pure consciousness. The Zohar explains that what first emerged was not physical water but the consciousness that is within water—the thought energy-intelligence of sharing or Chesed. On the Second Day, two disparate forms of consciousness emerged.

Humankind itself is divided—we do this, we do that—there are always two sides to every coin. Our problem is that we have left behind the consciousness of *Yom Echad*. It is my hope that, through understanding the true nature of water, as revealed in this section, we will re-connect with the consciousness of unity. However, this is dependent on humankind's actions.

Had Adam not fallen, not bound himself to duality, we would all still behave in the way of sharing. This does not mean we would be all the same, because everyone would share within his or her level of consciousness.

The seed of chaos began on the Second Day of Creation, when two opposing elements were created to co-exist. The Zohar explains that the Third Day of Creation set out to resolve the problem by becoming the filament (the balance) with the restrictions now imposed on Creation. In learning Kabbalah, and about the story of Creation, what we desire to achieve is a reconnection with the reality of unity, and that beautiful world of Beresheet One. We all innately have the *one* consciousness, which is to share.

The Meaning of Two

As we have explained, the seven days of Creation refer to the seven thought energy-intelligences of Chesed, Gevurah, Tiferet, Netzach, Hod, Yesod, and Malchut. The word *sheni* or "two," indicates that there is a division or separation. Gevurah is the energy-intelligence of Desire to Receive, a force that creates separation because it is desire that differentiates people. No two people have the same Desire to Receive, and these separate desires motivate us to do what we do. When we share with a common goal, this can unify everyone, but when our individual desires need to be met, this creates a separation, since we all have a separate and distinct desire.

There was a Desire to Receive on Day One, but it was unified by the seed. Separation occurs as something becomes manifest, becoming something other than it was originally. Each day of Creation represents another concept. Day Two represents the consciousness of separation, which is why it is called *sheni* or "two," a second thing. It is not as it once was in the seed. On Day Three, another concept came into being to unify the two separated forces—Desire to Share and Desire to Receive. This third force is called the Central Column or the Desire to Receive for the Sake of Sharing.

9 And God said, "Let the water under the heaven be gathered to one place, and let dry land appear." And it was so. 10 God called the dry land "Earth," and the gathered waters God called "seas." And God saw that it was good. 11 And God said, "Let the land put forth grass: seed-bearing plants and fruit-bearing trees, according to their various kinds." And it was so. 12 The land produced grass; plants bore seed according to their kinds and trees bore fruit with seed in it according to their kinds. And God saw that it was good. 13 And there was evening, and there was morning—Third Day. 14 And God said, "Let there be lights in the firmament of the heaven to separate the day from the night, and let them serve as signs to indicate the seasons and the days and the years, 15 and let them be lights in the firmament of the heaven to give light to the Earth." And it was so. 16 God made two great lights—the greater light to rule the day and the lesser light to rule the night. God also made the stars. 17 God set them in the firmament of the heaven to give light upon the earth, 18 to rule over the day and over the night, and to divide the light from the darkness. And God saw that it was good. 19 And there was evening, and there was morning—Fourth Day. 20 And God said, "Let the water teem with swarms of living creatures, and let birds fly above the earth across the firmament of heaven." 21 And God created the great creatures of the sea, and every creeping creature and moving

living thing with which the water teems, according to their kinds; and every winged bird according to its kind. And God saw that it was good. 22 And God blessed them and said, "Be fruitful and multiply and fill the water in the seas, and let the birds multiply on the earth." 23 And there was evening, and there was morning—Fifth Day. 24 And God said, "Let the land produce living creatures according to their kinds: cattle, and creatures that creep along the ground, and wild animals, each according to its kind." And it was so. 25 God made the wild animals according to their kinds, the cattle according to their kinds, and all the creatures that creep along the ground according to their kinds. And God saw that it was good.

It Was Good

The Bible says "and God saw that it was good"—but why did God need to evaluate all that He did? Did He think that perhaps He might have made a mistake and created something that was not good? Rav Shimon said that there is no anger or judgment in the statement "it was good." This reminds us that whatever will be, will be—whatever has to be done must be done without anger and without judgment. If we have this perspective, then our actions are always for the Light.

26 Then God said, "Let us make man in Our image, after Our likeness, and let them rule over the fish of the sea and the birds of the air, over the cattle, over all the earth, and over all the creatures that creep along the ground." 27 So God created man in His own image, in the image of God He created him; male and female He created them. 28 God blessed them and said to them, "Be fruitful and multiply; and replenish the earth and subdue it, and have dominion over the fish of the sea and the birds of the air and over every living creature that creeps on the ground." 29 And God said, "Behold, I have given you every seed-bearing plant on the face of the whole earth and every tree that has fruit with seed in it. They will be yours for food; 30 and to all the beasts of the earth and all the birds of the air and all the creatures that creep on the ground—wherein is a living soul—I give every green plant for food." And it was so. 31 And God saw all that He had made, and it was very good. And there was evening, and there was morning—Sixth Day.

Male and Female

Beresheet 1:27 says, *zachar unekeva Barah otam*, "male and female He created them." The Bible is not discussing Adam and Eve here, as is commonly understood, but rather the energy-intelligences of Desire to Share and Desire to Receive.

The thought energy-intelligence of sharing, code named *Zachar* (Male), creates the sperm. The thought energy-intelligence of receiving, code-named *Nukva* (Female), creates the ovum. The sperm gives life, expanding outward and sharing, while the ovum has the ability to capture, to draw and receive into itself the sperm. While we are not talking about Adam and Eve, there is no question that the thought energy-intelligence that would ultimately create Adam and Eve existed in potential.

Beresheet 2:1 And the Heavens and the Earth, in their vast array, were completed.

The Physical World is an Illusion

The Zohar says that when we discuss the first seven days, we are only referring to consciousness and the immaterial nature of the Bible. One percent is what the physical reality is made of, and the remaining 99 percent is the real world—the world of consciousness—which is not subject to the chaos we experience on the physical level. All the chaos we experience—cancer or a heart attack, for example—is of a purely physical nature. On the non-physical level there is no chaos, but because we have placed so much emphasis on the physical, it is difficult for us to come to this understanding. We are only familiar with the one percent physical aspect of life. From this perspective, we created psychology, where, after thirty years of therapy, an improvement in our self-knowledge may be seen.

There is only one true reality—and even physics has demonstrated that the material world is illusory. Gradually, science is beginning to realize that there must be something beyond its narrow scope of knowledge. This is the work of The Kabbalah Centres, where we are striving to get back to the world of reality, and to extract ourselves from this familiar physical playground. We are going to change things that have never been changed before. There is only one way we can do this—and it is when we see that this world and its chaos are illusions.

We need to understand that our old awareness is the obstacle. When we are stuck in old ways of thinking, how do we know what we are supposed to do? The ultimate conclusion is to come to the realization that the Zohar is correct—the physical reality is an illusion.

Why should we be able to walk through a wall? The wall was created to limit something of a physical nature. It is quite obvious that the wall is an obstacle for us, yet the physical world was not meant to be an impediment. The intent of Creation was not that we should suffer, but, looking at the evidence of pain and hardship throughout the world, how can we think otherwise?

The Zohar says that, if we do not start changing our consciousness, we will have to live with the resulting chaos. We will have to partake in the games of Satan's playing field. Satan has all the time in the world—and sooner or later he will get us with the ultimate chaos known as mortality. The Zohar assures us that there is a way out of this.

Within the creation of Heaven and Earth lies the secret. What Beresheet 1:1 teaches us is that there was no physical Heaven and Earth—they came later. The first verse is about two universes that existed on a potential level. For example, I think of what I want to do before I act; this thought exists on a potential level. This is not too difficult to understand but we forget this simple truth. Our egos flatter us into thinking everything is fine and we are in control, that we have dominion over our lives, and that there is no other alternative. This is the power of Satan, a force we have now begun to recognize. We need to know that every decision, whether it turns out to be a wise one or not, is not ours.

All the tools we have at our disposal, and the positive changes we undergo, are all because Kabbalah enables us to perceive the world and ourselves in a new way—thus we have changed, and our consciousness is different. The things we were so concerned with before no longer provide us with the same meaning that they once did.

2 And on the Seventh Day God had finished the work which He had made; and God rested on the Seventh Day from all His work, which He had made. 3 And God blessed the Seventh Day and made it holy, because on it He rested from all the work of creating that which He had made.

No Time, Space or Motion in the First Days of Creation

With this portion, we have the idea of the Sabbath. Christians have Sunday, Muslims have Friday, and the Jews have Saturday. Do traditionalists really think that God was too tired and so He needed a day of rest? It says, "God finished His work on the Seventh Day," which has never been open to interpretation. Did God work on the Seventh Day or did He not? The Bible says that God finished His work on the Seventh Day and rested on the Seventh Day, which does not make sense. How does one work and rest at the same time? Was this the thought behind God's declaration of the Sabbath?

All of these misinterpretations and corruptions have emerged for one reason—to prevent people from understanding the essential purpose of Beresheet. In the courses given at The Kabbalah Centres over the past fifty years, we have learned that God did not rest on Shabbat; He worked. God did not finish the universe until the Seventh Day.

We have learned that when the Bible said "and God rested" it did not mean that God was so overworked after creating the universe that He needed a day to rest.

Shabbat and the Seventh Day

If God finished His work on the Seventh Day, where did this
concept of resting come from? The most difficult day of the week
for me is Shabbat. I work the hardest on Shabbat—the other six
days are for rest. The Zohar says that God ended His work on
the Seventh Day (Shabbat) because He did not create *vayehi erev
vayehi boker*—there was no day and night, no positive and negative.
When these two aspects exist there is conflict. On Shabbat, we have
the benefit of enjoying a day without conflict, without a filament.
Throughout the mundane six days of the week, there is the quality
of *vayehi erev vayehi boker*, therefore we need a Central Column to
maintain the balance—as it is in a lightbulb. On Shabbat, there are
no two separate entities called positive and negative that need to
be united with a filament. On the Seventh Day, God created a new
concept—positive and negative as one unified whole—similar to
the first day of Creation but with one difference, on Shabbat it is in
a manifested state. *Yom Rishon* was in the potential state—Chesed
was the seed—it was unified. On Shabbat, in this physical
dimension, all we have to do to manifest this potential state is to
connect with it.

The word Shabbat comes from the Hebrew word *shvita*, meaning
"strike." He struck against something—refrained. He struck
against that which existed throughout the other six days of the
week—*vayhi erev vayhi boker*. On Shabbat, God created an aspect
that canceled out as two separate entities, the day and night factor
(positive and negative). Positive and negative became unified as
one whole.

Why does Beresheet Two begin with the Seventh Day of
Creation—is not Day Seven also part of Beresheet One, like the
other six days of Creation? It is, and it is not. Malchut (Day Seven)
is the end. The fruit is the end-product of a seed, but it is also

the beginning of a new tree because of its seed within. The fruit of Shabbat contains the seed for everything else. It is the end and the beginning—and everything is going to take place right there. Therefore, Day Seven is inserted in Beresheet Two because this is where the action is. Everything before Beresheet Two is all potential. On Day Seven (Malchut) things begin to move. There is an expression that says that from the *botz* or "mud," (where the action is), is where we get problems. The seed has to go through a process, a six-step process, and then Shabbat is the impact. What we do on Shabbat impacts the outcome of the next six days of the week.

4 These are the generations of the Heavens and the Earth when they were created, when the Lord God made the Earth and the Heavens,

The Six and the One

The Zohar explains that Beresheet is a code to tell us there is something before Creation. Beresheet 1:1 tells us about *Shamayim* (Six) and *haAretz* (One)—which are Zeir Anpin and Malchut. The Zohar says this verse encapsulates the secrets of why all of this came about. There was a clash between Zeir Anpin (sharing) and Malchut (receiving). It is a paradox because it is human nature to seek comfort, yet it is only through the clash that we can get this comfort.

First we have the development of the Six and the One, and then the clash, the impact, the Seventh Day, and from that came *adam* (man), who is made from Malchut, from the earth. Where did Eve come from? She came from Adam. First there is the male (a positive, sharing aspect), and from the male comes the female (a negative, receiving aspect). Positive is the cause, and negative is the effect.

Small Letter Hei

There is a small letter *Hei* [ה] in the word *behibaram* [בהבראם], "when they were created," which contains the same letters as the word "Abraham." This small letter *Hei* helps us connect to the energy of sharing. When we reduce our Desire to Receive, we connect to the energy of Abraham which is *chesed* (sharing).

5 no shrub of the field had yet appeared on the Earth and no plant of the field had yet sprung up, for the Lord God had caused it to rain upon the earth and there was no man to till the ground; 6 but a mist came up from the earth and watered the whole surface of the ground. 7 Then the Lord God formed man from the dust of the ground and breathed into his nostrils the breath of life; and the man became a living soul. 8 Now the Lord God had planted a garden in the east, in Eden; and there He put the man whom He had formed. 9 And the Lord God made all kinds of trees grow out of the ground—trees that were pleasing to the eye and good for food; and the Tree of Life in the middle of the garden, and the Tree of Knowledge of Good and Evil. 10 And a river flowed out from Eden to water the garden; from there it was parted and became four heads. 11 The name of the first is Pishon, which winds through the entire land of Havilah, where there is gold. 12 And the gold of that land is good; there is bedillium and stones of onyx. 13 The name of the second river is Gihon, which winds through the entire land of Cush. 14 The name of the third river is Tigris, which runs along the east side of Asshur. And the fourth river is the Euphrates. 15 The Lord God took the man and put him in the Garden of Eden to dress it and to keep it.

Beresheet Two

The Zohar, in Vayera 1:1-2 says:

> Rav Chiya opened the discussion, IT IS WRITTEN, "The
> flowers appeared on the earth, the time of the singing
> of the birds has come, and the voice of the turtledove is
> heard in our land." (Shir HaShirim 2:12) "The flowers
> appeared on the earth," MEANS THAT when the Holy
> One, blessed be He, created the world, He endowed the
> earth with appropriate powers, so that everything was in
> the earth BUT it did not produce any fruit until Adam was
> created. As soon as Adam was created, everything in the
> earth became visible, that is, the earth began to reveal the
> powers and products that were implanted within it. And
> then it was said, "The flowers appear on the earth."

> Similarly, the Heavens did not give any powers to the earth
> until humankind appeared, as it is written, "And no plant
> of the field was yet in the earth, and no herb of the field
> had yet grown, for the Lord, our God, had not caused it
> to rain upon the earth, and there was not a man to till the
> ground." (Beresheet 2:5). All the offspring and products
> were concealed in the earth. They did not appear, and the
> Heavens were prevented from pouring rain on the earth
> because humankind did not yet exist. Because it had not
> yet been created, the revelation of all things was delayed.
> As soon as humankind appeared, however, "The flowers
> appeared on the earth," and all the hidden and concealed
> powers were now revealed.

The passages quoted in the Zohar from Song of Songs refer to
Beresheet Two, which is where the actual, physical, corporeal
manifestation of Beresheet One is revealed. Beresheet One deals

with thought energy-intelligence, and nothing more. It identifies the true reality, the 99 percent of everything. For example, 99 percent of a table is not physical wood but thought energy-intelligence consisting of atoms. It is the 99 Percent Reality that we want to connect to, because the true reality is where everything exists, where all information exists, and where the cosmos actually exists.

When God created the world, He infused the earth with all the energy it would ever need, yet it did not produce any fruit whatsoever. The earth was there, the trees were there, everything was there, but until Adam was created everything remained in a state of suspended animation. The sun in Beresheet One was a sun that did not shine, yet had the potential to shine.

We learn from this Zohar portion that humankind controls the cosmos, controls everything both animate and inanimate in this universe. We should be able to stop the sun. According to the Zohar, it is not only Joshua but all of us who have the potential to perform such an action as stopping the sun in its path. Adam controlled the universe, and because we all come from Adam, everyone has the same power of control. But why do we not see it today? Does it really exist?

Physicists today, have come to the conclusion that if I am in New York and thinking of flying to California next week, and then walking on the beach there, my footprints will appear in the sand before I even land in California and start walking on that beach. The physicists admit that it is hard to understand how this could occur (footprints) when on a physical level the individual has not even arrived there yet. Yet with the quantum, time, space, and motion are an illusion. But can we really be in California, and enjoy the sun and sea fully as a thought, while we are still physically in

New York? Absolutely. Can we feel warm? Absolutely. We have just been so conditioned that we forget what true reality is all about.

According to the Zohar, humankind was created with total control of every situation in life—yet there could be two problems. First, we have to believe implicitly that this can be so. But, secondly, we are too susceptible to the views of others. For example, if the doctor tells us he can only promise a temporary relief, this means that we have to exclude the possibility that there can ever be permanent relief because the doctor has already said relief will be temporary. In our mind, we have established temporary relief, so this is all the relief we are ever going to get.

The Zohar says we are in control and, when we seek totality, this is what we get. But because we are so consumed in the world of the illusion of the five senses, we can never achieve that which we believe we want to achieve. In Beresheet Two, this condition was created. Nothing moves in this universe without humankind.

When Joshua stopped the sun, was it because he felt he could not otherwise defeat the enemy? Does it seem logical that a man who could create such a miracle as stopping the sun could not defeat an enemy? The Zohar explains that, in another frame of reference, Joshua needed the sun to shine so that he could tap into its energy. Whether it was night or daytime was not his problem. The sun is not just something physical that shines, it is a unique thought energy-intelligence. It is a power. Everything rotates around the sun.

Shabbatai Donolo, a famous Italian astrophysicist, astrologer, and physician (913-982 CE), investigated the sun and discovered that the reason everything rotates around it is because the sun consists of a balanced state of all the energies that exist in this universe—much like the electron that circles around the nucleus in an atom. The Zohar explains that the electron has a thought energy-intelligence of

Desire to Receive—it is always hungry and needs to keep tapping the energy of the nucleus. When the electron tries to get close to the nucleus, the aspect of restriction kicks in, which is why it keeps circling around the nucleus.

It is the same with the sun, without which we cannot exist. Joshua knew how to tap the power of the sun—but what he ostensibly knew was that everything in this universe is governed by laws and principles. He understood that nothing on a physical level can ever explain why things are the way they are.

Joshua wanted to tap the energy of balance and the Desire to Share to defeat his enemy, so he stopped nightfall, which is the energy-intelligence called "night, darkness" or Desire to Receive. He understood that, if darkness set in, the sun could not operate and would go back into suspended animation. Joshua took control of the internal energy of the sun and prevented it from ceasing to manifest itself, so even though it was nightfall, and he could not see the sun, the force of the sun functioned as it does during the day, and the moon stood still.

The Zohar says the Bible is only to provide us with information on how we can take control of our lives and the cosmos. We can relive the time before the sin of Adam, when he was in total control. In the *Ana Beko'ach* prayer, we recite specific *kavanot* or "meditations" on particular letters. What is the purpose of this? Why do the *Sefer Yetzirah* ("Book of Formation"), the Zohar, Rav Isaac Luria and all the kabbalists bring this to our attention? Rav Shimon says that in the Age of Aquarius, the days of the coming of Messiah, all this information will again be restored. Today, it is here in print, so no one can tell anyone else to study or not to study. It is not any longer a question about the availability of this information.

The reason we pray is because prayer is a system of connection; it is the channel by which we can actually control and dominate everything around us. Why would we want to operate on the 1 Percent Illusory Level of the five senses when we can tap into the 99 Percent True Reality? Kabbalah makes an attempt to bring out this potential of the individual by showing us how we can connect with things that are of the True Reality—where past, present, and future are all here now. The kabbalists make use of energy that is far superior to the physical connections.

Therefore, the Zohar explains that, whatever we want, whatever we desire, is what we get. We can close our eyes for a minute and be wherever we want to be, and have whatever we desire. The kabbalist also knows how to maintain such a state. It is not something fleeting or something that changes with each thought we have. Most of us think about everything we want and, perhaps, we get it for a minute. That is true for us today but we have a problem. How do we maintain it? How do we stay away from illusion? In *Talmud Eser Sefirot*, the Study of the Ten Luminous Emanations at the Kabbalah Centre, we learn the method by which we can capture and maintain what we receive. This is where, as they say, we separate the men from the boys.

16 And the Lord God commanded the man, saying: "Of every tree of the garden you may freely eat; 17 but of the Tree of Knowledge of Good and Evil you must not eat, for when you eat of it you will surely die." 18 The Lord God said, "It is not good for the man to be alone. I will make him a help meet." 19 And out of the ground the Lord God formed all the beasts of the field and all the birds of the air; and brought them to the man to see what he would name them; and whatever the man called each living creature, that would be its name. 20 And the man gave names to all the cattle, the birds of the air and all the beasts of the field; but for Adam there was not found a help meet. 21 And the Lord God caused the man to fall into a deep sleep; and while he slept, He took one of the man's ribs and closed up the place with flesh. 22 And from the rib that the Lord God had taken out of the man, He made a woman, and He brought her to the man. 23 The man said, "This is now bone of my bones and flesh of my flesh; she shall be called 'woman,' for she was taken out of man." 24 For this reason a man shall leave his father and mother and be united to his wife, and they will become one flesh. 25 And they were both naked, the man and his wife, and they were not ashamed.

Beresheet 3:1 Now the serpent was more subtle than any of the wild animals the Lord God had made. He said to the woman, "Did God really say, 'You must not eat from any tree in the garden'"? 2 And the woman said to the serpent, "Of the fruit from the trees in the garden we may eat, 3 but of fruit from the tree that is in the middle of the garden, God did say, 'You must not eat, and you must not touch it, or you will die.' " 4 And the serpent said to the woman, "You will not surely die 5 for God knows that when you eat of it your eyes will be opened, and you will be like God, knowing good and evil." 6 And when the woman saw that the tree was good for food and pleasing to the eye, and that the tree was to be desired to make one wise, she took of the fruit thereof and ate it, and she also gave some to her husband, who was with her, and he ate it.

The Tree of Life and the Tree of Knowledge

At this point in the story, we come to the creation of Adam and the manifestation of the Tree of Life and the Tree of Knowledge in the Garden of Eden. God told Adam—and note that, in Hebrew, the Bible does not indicate that He said *to* Adam, it says *on* Adam—not to partake of the Tree of Knowledge but only eat from the Tree of Life because the day he would eat from the Tree of Knowledge he would surely die. After we read the story of Adam and his relationship to the Tree of Life and the Tree of Knowledge, we are told that God said it is not good that Adam should be alone, that he needed a helper. Who was this helper for Adam? It was not Eve—and it was not, in fact, the story of the rib. We are told that God formed all of the animals and all the birds from the earth, in the same way He formed Adam, and then He brought the animals, birds, and everything to Adam so that he could name them. At this point in the Bible, we still have not reached the story of Eve. Only after Adam had named everything does the Bible then say that Adam could not find a suitable helper.

God put Adam to sleep and took one of his ribs, and thereby created Eve. Without going into the inconsistencies concerning the creation of Eve, we should not forget that they were both naked. Then we have the story of the snake. Who was actually there when God commanded Adam not to eat from the Tree of Knowledge? Not even the animals were present. There are many inconsistencies in this portion, which is why it is one of the most confusing sections of the entire Bible.

As we have discussed previously, the Ari and the Zohar explain that there were two Creations—Beresheet One and Beresheet Two. Beresheet One is the true reality, which we refer to as consciousness. Science now essentially says that 99 percent of reality is consciousness, and one percent is physical. The real you and me is consciousness. The more we understand consciousness and place the physical reality in its proper perspective, the closer we are to the Creation of Beresheet One. Even though the Bible says that there was day and night, in Beresheet One, One Day was not referring to the physical reality.

Rav Isaac Luria (the Ari) explains that the account of the first seven days of Creation is not referring to aspects of time, space, and motion. The Zohar says that the world was not created in seven days—days were not even a concept because there was no time, space, or motion at that point.

The Creation of Beresheet One concerns what is in the Upper Worlds, which is what the Study of the Ten Luminous Emanations is about—teaching us to go beyond the limitations of time, space, and motion. I have found that this study is the only one in existence that can elevate a human being to the consciousness necessary to understand concepts beyond time, space, and motion. The Bible helps us to understand that the physical reality suppresses the truth and leads us to the pitfalls of time, space, and motion.

In Beresheet One, we learn of the Seven Sefirot, and that, since each Sefira consists of another ten Sefirot, the amount of Sefirot is infinite because numbers only exist in the physical realm.

The real Adam and Eve were created in Beresheet One, and then placed into the physical reality, which is Earth. At one time they were pure and they had only the Desire to Receive for the Sake of Sharing. Then along came the Earth, with its Desire to Receive, a force that causes every person to think in terms of time, space, and motion.

The Zohar says that all of us were created in Beresheet One, in a realm beyond time, space, and motion but because Adam ate from the Tree of Knowledge, he placed his consciousness in an affinity with the physical reality. He succumbed to the temptation, to the Desire to Receive for the Self Alone, thereby taking on another consciousness, different from the one with which he was born. Through his action, Adam parted with the consciousness of Beresheet One. Keeping this in mind will help us come to terms with many of the subsequent inconsistencies.

By naming the animals, birds, and so on, Adam realized the difference between a speaking being and the other creaturely kingdoms. Adam named the animals for the purpose of understanding who he was himself. He understood that the consciousness of humankind differentiates humanity from all the other kingdoms because humans have a greater intensity of the Desire to Receive. Because of this desire, we can think of performing actions that an animal would never consider, actions such as traveling to New

York or anywhere else in the world. The Desire to Receive even differentiates one person from another. Someone like Napoleon or like Alexander the Great obviously had a greater Desire to Receive than most people.

The Desire to Receive should not be thought of as inherently negative, for it is this desire that can bring down the Endless Light. Moses had the greatest Desire to Receive, and therefore he also had the ultimate connection with the Lightforce of the Creator. This is what we learn from this section of the Bible—yet just to learn and not to derive some essential benefit is not the purpose of the Bible.

Free Will and Immortality

Adam and Eve were made to live forever. We know Adam and Eve did not die after eating of the Tree of Knowledge although God said they would. The Bible does not say that God said they would die, but rather *mimenu mot tamut* or "you will surely die," meaning death would ultimately prevail. Adam would have lived forever if he had not eaten from the Tree of Knowledge, instead he lived for a mere 930 years. After eating from the Tree of Knowledge, Adam was destined to live one thousand years—but he gave seventy years of his life to King David.

This story is an exercise of free will. God created humankind to exercise free will, and now, for the first time, He provided an opportunity for us to do so. Why did Eve choose to eat from the Tree of Knowledge after God forbade it? The Zohar interprets this as God's way of communicating that the working process of Creation requires both good and evil—*tov* is translated as "good" and *ra* means "evil," but the meaning more closely resembles positive and negative, like the poles in a battery that permit the current to flow, and where the negative is as vital as the positive.

There is no question of Adam and Eve dying as a consequence of eating the fruit. What they did was bring in something new to give to life—they brought in death.

7 And the eyes of both of them were opened, and they realized they were naked; so they sewed fig leaves together and made coverings for themselves. 8 And they heard the voice of the Lord God as He was walking in the garden in the cool of the day, and the man and his wife hid from the presence of the Lord God among the trees of the garden. 9 But the Lord God called to the man, "Where are you?" 10 He answered, "I heard Your voice in the garden, and I was afraid because I was naked; so I hid myself." 11 And God said, "Who told you that you were naked? Have you eaten from the tree that I commanded you not to eat from?" 12 The man said, "The woman You gave to be with me—she gave me of the tree, and I ate it." 13 Then the Lord God said to the woman, "What is this that you have done?" The woman said, "The serpent beguiled me, and I ate." 14 And the Lord God said to the serpent, "Because you have done this, cursed are you above all the cattle and all the wild animals! You will crawl on your belly and you will eat dust all the days of your life. 15 And I will put enmity between you and the woman, and between your offspring and hers; they will bruise your head, and you will strike their heel." 16 To the woman He said, "I shall greatly increase your pains in childbearing; with pain you shall give birth to children. Your desire shall be for your husband, and he will rule over you." 17 And to Adam He said, "Because you listened to your wife and ate from the tree

about which I commanded you, 'You must not eat of it,' cursed is the ground because of you; through painful toil you shall eat of it all the days of your life. 18 It shall bring forth thorns and thistles for you and you shall eat the plants of the field. 19 By the sweat of your brow shall you eat bread until you return to the ground, since from it you were taken; for dust you are and to dust you shall return." 20 Adam named his wife Eve, because she would become the mother of all the living. 21 The Lord God made garments of skin for Adam and his wife and clothed them. 22 And the Lord God said, "The man has now become like one of Us, knowing good and evil. He must not be allowed to reach out his hand and take also from the Tree of Life and eat, and live forever." 23 So the Lord God banished him from the Garden of Eden to work the ground from which he had been taken. 24 So He drove the man out, and He placed on the east side of the Garden of Eden cherubim and a flaming sword flashing back and forth to guard the way to the Tree of Life.

Eve, the Snake and Taking Responsibility

What is the true meaning of the story of the snake? It is about negative energies in this universe and how to overcome them. A snake cannot attack a person; it must be motivated from another place. A cobra cannot attack without a command from Above on the spiritual level. All the physical chaos that humanity must undergo is because of negative energy created by the self.

Satan is an effect of human negativity, of negative consciousness. The Zohar says Satan was created because Adam and Eve could not truly exist until there was a manifestation of negative consciousness. Free will can only exist when there is a choice of doing things one way or another. The door to negativity was open, and Eve walked through. Why would she choose negativity? Why would someone want to give up a life in eternity for a world of problems?

The Zohar says no one else is responsible for our chaos. We cannot remove chaotic conditions if we do not perceive them from the non-observable level. We need to learn that it is our own actions that bring either blessings or chaos into our lives. In other words, we are responsible for everything that happens to us. In the portion of Beresheet we are at the seed level of this consciousness.

Beresheet 4:1 And Adam knew his wife Eve, and she conceived and gave birth to Cain. She said, "I have brought forth a man with the help of God." 2 And again she gave birth to his brother Abel. And Abel was a keeper of sheep, and Cain tilled the soil. 3 In the course of time Cain brought some of the fruits of the soil as an offering to God. 4 And Abel brought the first born of his flock and the fat portions thereof. And God looked with respect on Abel and his offering, 5 but on Cain and his offering He did not look with respect. So Cain was very angry, and his face was downcast. 6 Then God said to Cain, "Why are you angry? Why is your face downcast? 7 If you do well, will it not be lifted up? But if you do not do well, sin is crouching at the door; it desires to have you, but you must master it." 8 And Cain spoke to his brother Abel, and it came to pass while they were in the field that Cain attacked his brother Abel and killed him. 9 And God said to Cain, "Where is your brother Abel?" And he said, "I don't know, am I my brother's keeper?" 10 And He said, "What have you done? The voice of your brother's blood cries out to me from the ground. 11 And now you are cursed from the ground, which opened its mouth to receive your brother's blood from your hand. 12 When you till the ground, it will no longer yield its crops for you. You will be a restless wanderer on the Earth." 13 Cain said to God, "My punishment is more than I can bear. 14 Behold, today You have driven me from

the land, and Your presence will be hidden from me; I shall be a fugitive and wanderer on the earth, and whoever shall find me shall slay me." 15 And God said to him, "If anyone slays Cain, he will suffer vengeance sevenfold." Then God put a mark on Cain lest anyone who finds him shall slay him. 16 And Cain went out from the presence of God and lived in the land of Nod, east of Eden.

Cain and Abel

Before Cain, there was no concept of murder. Yet Cain had never witnessed any killing, so how did he know he was capable of it? There was no concept of death at this time, either, so how did Cain even have the thought that Abel needed to die?

It says in the Zohar that Cain bit Abel's neck and burst his main artery—and this is how Abel was killed. In the spelling of the words "bite" and "kiss" in Hebrew there is a difference of only one letter—*Kuf* and *Chaf*—*neshika* means "kiss" and *neshicha* means "bite." With a kiss we close our lips—there is restriction—but to bite we must open our lips.

The lips are the *masach* (curtain or restriction). The way to receive the Light is only by restricting it, and if we receive directly without restriction we create a short circuit. Cain killed Abel with a bite, with an open mouth and no lips—therefore no restriction was present. This was the difference between Cain and Abel.

Cain was from the Left Column and he drew the Light directly, which caused his brother's death. When he bit Abel, he did not use his lips to reject the Light. By drawing the Light with no restriction not only does this show Cain's nature but it also shows that he killed Abel without knowing that he had done so. Cain had no intention of killing his brother—he did not even know what death was. However, Cain was jealous and wanted to draw the Light of Wisdom directly. This is the same way that an overload of electricity can cause a short circuit with the potential to kill. Such a short circuit is what caused the death of Abel.

17 And Cain knew his wife, and she conceived and gave birth to Enoch. And he built a city, and he named it after his son Enoch. 18 To Enoch was born Irad, and to Irad was born Mehujael, and to Mehujael was born Methushael, and to Methushael was born Lamech. 19 Lamech married two women, one named Adah and the other named Zillah. 20 Adah gave birth to Jabal; he was the father of those who live in tents and raise cattle. 21 His brother's name was Jubal; he was the father of all who play the harp and flute. 22 Zillah also bore a son, Tubal-Cain, who forged all kinds of tools out of bronze and iron. Tubal-Cain's sister was Na'amah. 23 Lamech said to his wives, "Adah and Zillah, listen to me; wives of Lamech, hear my words. I have slain a man for wounding me, a young man for hurting me. 24 If Cain is avenged sevenfold, then truly Lamech seventy-seven times." 25 Adam knew his wife again, and she gave birth to a son and named him Seth. She said, "God has granted me another child instead of Abel, whom Cain slew." 26 And to Seth also a son was born, and he named him Enosh. Then men began to call on the name of the Lord.

Beresheet 5:1 This is the Book of the Generations of Adam. In the day that God made man, He made him in the likeness of God. 2 He created them male and female and blessed them. And He called their name Adam. 3 When Adam had lived 130 years, he had a son in his own likeness, in his own image; and he named him Seth. 4 And after Seth was born, Adam lived 800 years and had other sons and daughters. 5 And the days that Adam lived were 930 years, and then he died. 6 And Seth lived 105 years, and he bore Enosh. 7 And after he became the father of Enosh, Seth lived 807 years and had other sons and daughters. 8 And the days that Seth lived were 912 years, and then he died. 9 When Enosh had lived 90 years, he bore Kenan. 10 And after he became the father of Kenan, Enoch lived 815 years and had other sons and daughters. 11 And the days that Enosh lived were 905 years, and then he died. 12 When Kenan had lived 70 years, he bore Mahalalel. 13 And after he became the father of Mahalalel, Kenan lived 840 years and had other sons and daughters. 14 And the days Kenan lived were 910 years, and then he died. 15 When Mahalalel had lived 65 years, he bore Jared. 16 And after he became the father of Jared, Mahalalel lived 830 years and had other sons and daughters. 17 And the days that Mahalalel lived were 895 years, and then he died. 18 When Jared had lived 162 years, he bore Enoch. 19 And after he became the father of Enoch, Jared lived 800 years and had other sons and daughters. 20 And the days that Jared lived were 962 years, and then he died. 21 When Enoch had lived 65 years, he bore Methuselah. 22 And after he became the father of Methuselah, Enoch walked with God 300 years and had other sons and daughters. 23 And the days that Enoch lived were 365 years. 24 Enoch walked with God; then he was no more, because God took him away. 25 And Methuselah lived 187 years, and he bore Lamech. 26 And after he became the father of Lamech, Methuselah lived 782 years and had other sons and daughters. 27 And the days Methuselah lived were 969 years, and then he died. 28 When Lamech had lived 182 years, he had a son. 29 He named him Noah and said, "He will comfort us in the labor and painful toil of our hands caused by the ground the Lord has cursed." 30 After Noah was born, Lamech lived 595 years and had other sons and daughters. 31 All the days Lamech lived were 777 years, and then he died. 32 And Noah was 500 years old, and Noah became the father of Shem, Ham, and Japheth.

Beresheet 6:1 And it came to pass, when men began to increase in number on the face of the earth and daughters were born to them, 2 the sons of God saw that the daughters of men were fair, and they took them for wives all of them they chose. 3 Then the Lord said, "My Spirit will not always strive with man, for he is also flesh; yet his days shall be a hundred and twenty years." 4 There were Nephilim (giants) on the earth in those days—and also afterward—when the sons of God went to the daughters of men and had children by them. They were the mighty men of old, men of renown. 5 And God saw how great

man's wickedness on the earth had become, and that every inclination of the thoughts of his heart was only evil continually. 6 And the Lord repented that He had made man on the earth, and His heart was filled with grief. 7 And the Lord said, "I will destroy mankind, whom I have created, from the face of the earth—both man and beast, and creatures that creep along the ground, and birds of the air—for it repents Me that I have made them." 8 But Noah found grace in the eyes of the Lord.

Back to the Beginning

We come to Shabbat to listen to the Bible reading of Beresheet so that we have the opportunity for another beginning. The seven days of Creation are only a metaphor. We have learned that we are not discussing them literally. We know that every word in the Bible is a code, and slowly, we draw these codes from concealment so they can assist us in removing the chaos that has continued since the sin of Adam.

Beresheet is the most important portion of the entire Bible. Here we have the opportunity to plant the seed that enables us to connect to the dimension that is free from all forms of chaos. It is in Beresheet that the first Seven Sefirot or levels of consciousness are developed. When consciousness emerged, these seven aspects were pure, without limitation, without chaos. Thus when we read about the first Seven Days of Creation on Shabbat, we combine the first Seven Sefirot to show the continuity. All of the other portions that follow Beresheet are tools that we can use to reach the dimension above time, space, and motion.

Beresheet is the beginning. We are given an opportunity with this reading to penetrate the seed. If we find that the seed is filled with chaos, we should know that negativity only exists to give us the potential to make changes. Once the seed has been planted and the branches have emerged, it is not the same. Try to think of it as pre-natal spiritual surgery.

Medical science concedes that, to date, it has not been able to discover the cause of cancer. It is obvious to an oncologist that a cancer did not begin with the tumor—it began perhaps thirty years earlier. Science cannot penetrate the seed of this disease because it does not have the tools to do so, it is that simple. Beresheet is about detecting what will emerge from the seed. With this portion, we hold in our hands our own beginning, the seed of everything that pertains to our life, everything that is to come throughout the year. Our aim is to maintain dominion over this seed for the next week or even the next six months. The reading of Beresheet is our opportunity to do just that.

Kabbalah is so simple. It is not full of confusion and contradiction like religion. Therefore, when we take in this reading on Shabbat, our consciousness should be directed in this way—towards simple truth. We have the merit to receive this blessing of information from the Zohar when we connect with this reading.

Beresheet is about taking control and being aware that Satan will try his best to wrest it from us because he wants us in his playing field. If we maintain a position in union with the seed, there is no chaos. Our own personal beginnings do not originate at the time of Creation. Perhaps they only began a few decades ago, yet we, too, have tools to help us go back to our beginning, to our personal Beresheet.

Summation and Conclusions

It is from this verse in Beresheet that one of the greatest controversies regarding the Bible emerged—creationism versus evolution. When the Torah Scroll came into its physical manifestation, over three thousand years ago, the kabbalists knew that it contained the technology of transformation. It was only later that it was turned into the major component of religion. This stands in the way of the Bible being utilized as a tool that can enable us to remove chaos. Some people who are against the teaching of Kabbalah—I call them "anti-kabbalists"—say, "Torah is Torah and the Zohar is a philosophy." We say no, it is more than that; it is the actual technology.

Why are there seven days of Creation? Who thought of the idea of a seven-day-week, and decided how to divide it? With the divisions of the month, I can understand that there is a physical parallel, one which follows the cycles of the moon. For most people, the days of the week are nothing more than something that appears on a calendar. Most of us do not question where a seven-day-week comes from. As we discussed previously, the different days are dealing with specific powerful energies of the Lightforce of God that appear as Sefirot or different levels of consciousness.

To remove all of the questions raised by the discrepancies of this portion would alone take up several chapters. One of these discrepancies is that on the Sixth Day, God created man: male and female. Is there anyone who ever thought this did not refer to Adam and Eve? Was there anyone else there at that time? Are we still under the impression that the Sixth Day is when God created male and female? Later in the portion we come to the section that states, "He created Adam from the dust of the Earth, and breathed into him a living soul." This is followed by the story of Eve, formed from Adam's rib. This does not make sense, since male and female were created on the Sixth Day. We could and do raise many more questions in this vein. What is not apparent, if you only focus on the literal version of the story, is that Beresheet is the seed of all technology.

Beresheet is always read following the connections of Sukkot and before the month of Scorpio. When we study Beresheet, we learn how the world came about. The story consists mainly of the creation of Adam and Eve and the subsequent sin of eating from the Tree of Knowledge.

Beresheet has been so misunderstood because what is written in it has so many inconsistencies. It is no wonder that science has disregarded the description of Creation, and even the Bible itself.

According to the Bible, the world was created in seven days about six thousand years ago, while science posits that the world is billions of years old and formed slowly over eons. How can the description of Creation in the Bible be compared with what is currently known by science? I accept the scientific point of view, and agree that the world is many billions of years old. Having accepted this, I would go even further and say the timespan is more like trillions of years. How can we know for sure what is correct? After all, what is a billion years? Perhaps beyond a thousand years we are dealing with another dimension? Science is unreliable. Although they seem to be precise, Einstein proved that all measurements are relative to the position of the measurer.

What is left to us, then, in the way of truth? There is nothing but the Bible, which, as I have said, contains inconsistencies that cause much misunderstanding. All of these inconsistencies are obvious for those who read even a little Hebrew. Rav Isaac Luria (the Ari), in the Writings of the Ari, and the Zohar both clearly describe these inconsistencies—one of which concerns the creation of Adam and Eve. The Bible says that, on the Sixth Day of Creation, "God created man in His own image, in the image of God He created him; male and female He created them." Who did God create? If we read any translation, *them* still refers to Adam and Eve, and yet Eve is only created later, in Beresheet 1:22. The Ari asks how we can reconcile these two statements. The Bible also says that after Adam was created, he was a body without a soul, and God then instilled a breath of life into his body.

Beresheet is the Keter, the seed. Whatever seeds we plant when we connect with this reading are what will grow for us in the future. We are not studying this portion simply to read a narrative of the events that occurred, nor do we come to the Kabbalah Centres for the purpose of practicing without an understanding of how it will personally benefit us.

BOOK OF BERESHEET:

Portion of Noah

PORTION OF NOAH

Introduction to Noah

In the portion of Noah, the Bible provides an historical account not only of Noah's time but also of all the events from Creation until the conclusion of the forty years in the wilderness. Many people are concerned with history, myself included, and yet we repeat history over and over again, not learning from our own experience. We do not study the Bible merely for historical or even traditional purposes but rather to gain support from, and understanding of, the 99 Percent Reality that Kabbalah can provide. Kabbalah teaches us that the Bible is eternally relevant and speaks to the present day of each and every generation.

Beresheet 6:9 These are the generations of Noah. Noah was a righteous man, and perfect in his generation, and Noah walked with God.

The Righteous and the World to Come

We have all probably learned about Noah and the Ark as little children. Is this simply a Bible story or does it contain a cosmic message—is there something more we can draw out from the portion of Noah? For deeper insight, we turn to the portion of Noah in the Zohar, which tells us that, contrary to the interpretation of the religious authorities on the phrase concerning righteousness, everyone has a portion in the World to Come. Religion, on the other hand, tells us that we only inherit the World to Come if we have been good—that righteous people are the only ones who will inherit this beautiful paradise. Yet if someone sins, how do they obtain a portion in the World to Come, and how are they immediately connected? In Rav Ashlag's commentary on the Zohar, he explains that *Alma De'ati* or the World of Reality is here right now—the World to Come does not mean something in the future. If it was referring to something in the future it would be called *Alma De'atida*, the World of the Future. In the Hebrew language, sometimes two different words can share the same meaning. The Hebrew *Alef Bet* is energy. According to *Sefer Yetzirah* ("Book of Formation"), the world was created through the Hebrew *Alef Bet*. For example, the letter *Bet* created the planet Saturn. Words that consist of this alphabet each contain a very definitive and distinct thought energy-intelligence.

The words *Olam Haba* (World to Come) do not mean the future world, the world of tomorrow—they refer to the world that is here now. The Hebrew word for "world" is *olam*, derived from the word *ne'elam*, meaning "concealed" or "invisible." *Olam Haba* is the world that exists beyond the five senses—it is the reality of existence that we do not want to deal with and thus continue to push aside. The Zohar says that we all have a portion in *Olam Haba*. The fact that we are alive means that we are connected to this world. But connection to this world is no guarantee that we are conscious of its existence. It is like a letter that needs to be opened and read. We can touch the envelope, read where it has come from, and know that there is a message for us inside—but we do not want to deal with it now. Are we connected with the letter? Yes, in the sense that we can touch and feel it, we are.

The Zohar says, "Praiseworthy are those who are *dealing* with Torah" because the words *osek betorah* do not mean "he studies Torah," but rather that "he deals with Torah." What a corruption the literal interpretation is. There is an impression that we have to *study* the Bible, and yet we can read the Bible day in and day out and not be connected with the physical words that have been expressed therein.

The World to Come comes to us, and it even becomes part of us—so we have to deal with it. The reason we "deal with the Torah" is because we are told in the Bible that we should deal with those things of which we are not conscious. As some physicists tell us, if we are not conscious of something, it does not exist. When we do not deal with the Bible, there is no connection.

The Zohar is discussing a radical concept here. The Zohar says that we have to *know* the ways of the Torah—it does not say we have to *fulfill* the ways of the Torah or be obedient—because knowing is the way we are going to make a connection. Therefore, we are all connected but this does not mean we are all conscious of our connection.

The Bible says that Noah was a *tzadik*, a righteous person. What is a righteous person? Is it someone who is right all the time and never wrong? No. The Talmud says: "There is no one so righteous in the entire world, who does only good and does not sin." So what is a righteous person, and why do we refer to someone as righteous? Furthermore, both the Talmud and the Zohar say that there is no such thing as being right or wrong. There were two leading sages of the early First Century CE, Shammai and Hillel, who each founded schools of opposing spiritual thought and, whenever there was a quarrel between them, they were both right. The Zohar questions how they could both be right. Surely it is either yes or no, is it not—because there is only one reality? The Zohar then reveals that reality depends on where you are coming from—it depends upon your perspective.

It is explained that the School of Shammai would say "not permitted" and the School of Hillel would say "permitted." The School of Shammai was hard on people, whereas the School of Hillel was more lenient. The Zohar explains that Shammai was very wealthy, and his internal characteristic—his soul—stemmed from the Left Column, which is Desire to Receive. Hillel, on the other hand, was poor, and his internal characteristic, his soul, stemmed from the Right Column, the sharing aspect. Hillel was so poor that he could not afford to pay for tuition, so he would climb onto the roof the school of learning and listen to the lessons through a skylight. The man who had nothing to give was lenient, and the one who had everything to share was stricter—what a paradox. The Zohar explains that, although they came from different frames of reference and observed the world through their own internal soul process—Hillel from the Right Column and Shammai from the Left Column—they were both *tzadikim* (righteous people).

According to the Zohar, humanity establishes that which is. If we see a chair, then the chair exists. If we do not see the chair, then it does not exist. It is the same principle with our internal characteristic. If we are negative, everything around us is negative because we have established that kind of magnetic field all around ourselves – and it can extend across the planet. Quantum physics tells us that everything is connected, everything is relative, and it all depends on where we are coming from, our perspective. It all depends on the individual. This is why we should never judge another person. There is no such thing as a righteous person in this physical, corporeal world—a person who does only good, in a general sense, and who does not sin because there is a purpose to existence. And, sooner or later, there must come a test—meaning an opportunity to elevate ourselves.

This is what the *tzadik* is about. Righteous does not mean that he or she is always right because they could be wrong. If we are connected with ourselves, and know ourselves, then we do not judge others, because, when we know ourselves, we also know that everyone has their own particular inner composition. A *tzadik* is one who understands that, unless we can become this other individual, feel what they feel, understand the way they understand, we cannot judge. A *tzadik* would ask how he can judge another person if he is in one frame of reference, and they are in another.

The obvious question in our minds is what it means to be connected to oneself? I am here and I exist, so am I not connected to myself? As it is in the connection of the *Amida*—which is the perfect place to be disconnected—there are times when we can be in a thousand other places, and we just rattle off the words, not even conscious of what we are saying. What a phenomenon.

This aspect within a human being is necessary because, without these opportunities, we would not grow and develop. Depending on how we look at them, problems can also be opportunities.

Everything in this universe can be good for one and bad for another. It depends on how we observe a situation.

When the Bible calls someone like Noah a *tzadik*, it is because they are connected with themselves. Failure is not a sign of not being righteous. Within this universe, and within us, there is another force. The reason we have two arms is to indicate that there is a right and a left aspect to us. There are many parts of the body that are divided into two parts, right and left, because balance depends on humanity alone. There is no inbuilt structure—as there is in a lightbulb—that makes balance between right and left. Man is the only creature that has a Right and a Left—because it is up to our discretion alone whether or not we create a balance between the two. We can either create an overcharge of energy or else we can create too little—it all depends on us. But, if we are connected, we will create the balance.

The Purpose of Life on Earth

The biblical commentators ask why it is said that Noah was a "*tzadik* (righteous person) in his generation." One commentary states that, had Noah lived in Abraham's generation, he would not have been considered righteous. He was honest, he did not steal, nor did he kill. But as he was building the Ark, knowing that everyone would die, he did not really care. He was comfortable. The Hebrew word for "comfort" is *noach*—which is why he was called Noah. Noah was not like Abraham, who pleaded for the people of Sodom. The Creator did not want to destroy the world completely because He knew that everything would simply repeat itself—even if He began Creation anew. Since there was no other decent man around at the time, Noah was selected for this task.

It is said that there were ten generations separating Noah from Abraham, but, in reality, all that had occurred during this span of time took place in the course of one week—because people essentially do not change. It is very difficult to change. Even good people, those who seek to do no evil, find it hard to change. A man is capable of abandoning his wife in a moment for the sake of his Desire to Receive for the Self Alone—which could even cause him to abandon his children too, if he felt any discomfort with his situation. In a moment of feeling discomfort—which is the exact opposite of *noach*—one is even capable of selling one's parents.

What do we leave behind us, besides a tombstone bearing our name? After our passing, there may not be anyone, not even a relative or neighbor, who will remember us. What do we truly leave behind? Each of us should strive to leave behind at least one other person who has changed because of our presence in their life. This is what it means truly to leave something behind.

Was Noah Righteous?

The Apta Rebbe (Rav Avraham Yehoshua Heshel of Apt, 1748-1825) asked, "Why engage at all in discussing whether or not Noah was righteous in his generation? Why say had he lived in Abraham's generation he would not have been so righteous? Why speak of him pejoratively when we can speak of him as a righteous man?"

The answer provided by the Apta Rebbe was that this was Noah's opinion of himself. Noah believed that, had he been living in Abraham's generation, he would not really have been righteous—and this means Noah was also humble. The entire story about Noah relates to human consciousness—consciousness establishes everything, and *is* everything. There may be a table, a chair or a car but science claims that, in theoretical terms, the question as to whether all of these objects are real is a matter of perception. If I think I already possess something or I am sure I have the ability to succeed with an endeavor, then there will be no impediment. This is why Noah was always saying that there will be no flood. He thought that, in this way, he would prevent it from happening.

The generation of the Flood did not, in fact, believe there would be a flood or that the Ark would save them—so they did not come to it. As a rule, if one believes that something negative will not happen, it will not—it is mind over matter. On the other hand, a person can also think everything is all right and be sorely mistaken.

It is easy for many to forget the importance of Shabbat. I am not trying to convince people that they have to come to the Kabbalah Centres on Shabbat. And yet, when someone misses several Shabbat connections, it is because they feel they already have the protection of the Light, and thus simply do not need to attend. They believe they already have what they need. People forget that one can lose everything in a minute—health, family, livelihood, the lot. Forgetfulness is one of our greatest enemies. Even after a person has been part of a Kabbalah Centre for ten years, they can still forget everything it meant to them in a single moment. Suddenly they discover what they think is wrong with their Centre. Suddenly everything seems to be a problem—but what about the time when that person truly believed their life changed for the better because of their connection to the Centre? One must then consider that perhaps it is not true—or possibly they are not seeing the whole picture.

In the next portion of Lech Lecha, we will read that Abraham pleaded with God when he heard that God was going to put an end to Sodom and Gomorrah because of their evil. Why should those who are *not* evil also suffer? Abraham asked God that, if he was able to find ten righteous men, would God save the city. But Abraham could not find even one righteous man. Many commentators have noted that Noah did not plead for his own generation. When the Angel of Death appears to the people, even the righteous will suffer without the methodology to protect themselves and their environment.

10 Noah had three sons: Shem, Ham, and Japheth. 11 The earth was also corrupt before God and the earth was full of violence. 12 God looked upon the earth and saw it was corrupt, for all flesh had corrupted their ways upon the earth. 13 And God said to Noah, "The end of all flesh is come before Me for the earth is filled with violence because of them. And behold I will destroy them with the earth. 14 Make yourself an ark of gopher wood; make rooms in it and coat it with pitch inside and out. 15 And this is how you are to fashion it: The length of the ark shall be 300 cubits, the breadth of it 50 cubits, and the height of it 30 cubits. 16 A roof you will make to the ark and in a cubit you will finish it above. And a door you will set in the side of the ark; with lower, middle, and upper decks you will make it. 17 And behold I am going to bring a flood of waters upon the earth from under the heavens, to destroy all flesh wherein there is the breath of life, and everything that is in the earth shall die.

The Ark as a Protective Energy Field

God told Noah to build an ark because He was about to destroy the entire world. The Zohar says that the first thing we should remember is that the Bible is not just an historical account, but that, each and every year when this reading takes place, there is something for us in the present time.

According to the Zohar, the ark was not a boat. The Bible includes many dimensions in the construction, which were not those of a ship. The word *teiva* means "box," and also "word." The Hebrew word for "boat" is *onia*. The Zohar explains that the dimensions of the Ark provide us with the means of protection—a security shield. There was no ship then. There was no wood. With all the specific dimensions mentioned, the Bible is referring to dimensions of Sefirot, thereby showing us how to tap into different levels of the Lightforce of God. Rav Shimon explains that *teiva* refers to a thought energy-intelligence of Malchut, our physical reality.

Noah created a security shield of thought energy-intelligence. Can we be saved by a thought? Yes, we can. We use thoughts to determine how to extricate ourselves from a problem. Noah created the first safety-net of intelligent thought. The measurements of the Ark are not connected to a physical entity, and the Ark in the story of Noah does not refer to a boat the way an engineer or an architect might conceive it. The dimensions mentioned in the Bible are the codes by which you and I today can create our own security shield. Every person has a magnetic field surrounding them. The Ark and its measurements are the technology by which we can protect ourselves.

The Consciousness of Water

The portion of Noah tells us that, because of human negativity, the Earth became polluted, and was consequently destroyed. What did the Earth do, in terms of negative activity, to cause the Great Deluge? Why does the Bible say that the Earth was polluted before God? It was humankind who polluted the Earth with their negativity.

The Zohar says that the Bible is actually clarifying the reality of existence—that a corrupt people could create a flood. Insurance companies cover damage, except for what they call "an act of God"—but there is no such thing as an act of God that creates a calamity. We are told that the people of Noah's generation were corrupt, and that, because of their negative deeds, God decided to destroy them—but nothing could be further from the truth. Positive actions create positive results, and negative actions create negative results. Today, we are destroying our environment, and, along with it, every living thing in this world. There will come a time when we will have no fruits or vegetables to eat, and no one will drink tap water anymore. Our own times are not unlike the generation of the Flood. The world has become a hostile environment. What we are beginning to eat now is genetically altered, and it has been suggested that these modified foods will soon replace real fruits and vegetables.

We are responsible for our environment, as were the people in Noah's time. Because they were corrupt, their influence was felt in the water. The natural character of water is sharing, and it has the ability to rise above the force of gravity—the consciousness of drawing to itself. The Earth draws everything toward itself: The consciousness of the Earth is to draw into its belly everything that exits. The Zohar says that water is a counterbalance to the force of gravity, which is the Desire for the Self Alone.

If the consciousness of water is one of sharing, how could it create such a vast devastation as the Flood? There is only one definition of God, and that is the Lightforce, which has an entirely positive nature and a character of sharing, along with the desire to enlighten. An electrical current can be used for destruction or for light. It is we, not God, who decide how to make use of it.

The Bible is revealing to us that human beings have the power to rule over physical reality. God did not transform the character of the water to become negative, to become a flood—it was the inhabitants of the Earth who were responsible for that devastation. The critical mass of negativity reversed the intrinsic nature of water from one of sharing into a destructive force. Human consciousness is what causes any change in physical reality.

From what the Bible tells us, we know that Noah was righteous. And we know that Noah built a security shield for himself and for his family. From this, we can understand that every person today should be striving to be righteous for their own benefit. The existence of morals and ethics in society proves only that we are prone to corruption. What the Zohar addresses is not morals or ethics, but how to be righteous and develop our own integrity. Righteousness is the means to enhance our own well-being; it is, in fact, for a seemingly selfish purpose. If we each transform our nature from greed to sharing, the first benefit would be the end of a corrupt society. Instead, we would have a world where everyone would treat each other with consideration and human dignity.

The Zohar says Satan convinced us to follow the rules. At the Kabbalah Centres, we do not use words like "service" or "prayer" because we attend and perform spiritual connections purely for ourselves—and not to serve or to pray to God. The Bible exists to provide us with the information to benefit ourselves. We should all want to become righteous people. Everyone knows that stealing or not paying taxes is possible. If you legitimately owe taxes, pay them, because you will get back more money. Do not look for a reason to avoid paying taxes—it pays to be correct.

The Zohar explains that humankind can discover that the chaos, pain, and suffering we endure are an illusion. It is real to us only because we have not come to understand that we are responsible for everything in our lives—both good and bad.

When did the Flood take place? It could only happen in the month of Scorpio, which is a water sign. Water is the one element in the world that is unified—it is Chesed. As was discussed in the portion of Bersheet, water is the most important element, and we can restore it to its rightful place, where it was before the corruption of Adam. When we connect with this reading we can change our entire environment.

We know that the dimensions of the Ark indicate the energy of the Lightforce that will emerge as we read the Torah Scroll on Shabbat. Even those not familiar with this teaching will receive the energy that is revealed by the Hebrew letters that comprise the words of this reading.

The Events of the Flood

What exactly happened during the Flood? For a long time, we have believed that it was simply the story of a man named Noah, who was told to enter the Ark and be saved from a flood that would descend upon the entire world. In my opinion, there was no Ark—at least not an ark in the strict sense of the term, which is a ship. An Ark is, in fact, the place housing Torah Scrolls. That all the creatures and everything that existed on Earth would come to Noah's Ark is an illusion perpetrated now for three thousand years. Yet there is something else that makes this story even more incredible. Besides destroying everything in its path, the Flood was bolstered by volcanic geysers erupting from deep within the core of the Earth—and these were also devastating. These geysers were so hot that neither rain nor water could cool them. It was so hot that skin and flesh melted. Yet we are expected to believe that people and animals survived because they lived on a ship—and that this little ship also survived?

The Nature of the Ark

As stated previously, the form of the Ark was the materialized system of the Sefirot—it was a realization of that structure, just as the designs of the Tabernacle and the Altar were. Thus the Ark was not only for Noah and his family—it had to be created for the defence of the entire world.

There have been many expeditions attempting to prove the historical veracity of the story of Noah. A great deal of time and money has been spent, but nothing has been found. I agree with the scientists that, perhaps, it never existed—although the Bible says it did. Many things in the Bible are contradictory. The Zohar considers the stories of the Bible to be tools to support us in our lives. In the first verse of this portion, it says, "these are the offspring of Noah; he was righteous and God was with him." Then it details his children—although the history is not very consistent.

The text next tells us that the Flood began on the 17th day of Cheshvan—the month of Scorpio. We know that the month of Scorpio is dedicated to water—which is why the portion of Noah will always be read in this month. The people of the generation of Noah did not only sin in the month of Cheshvan, they sinned throughout the year—and their negative acts polluted all water. The kabbalistic explanation for this is that it was not God who punished with the Flood—it was the consciousness of humanity that created all of the negative energy.

The kabbalistic understanding is that humankind infected the water with their own negative consciousness—in the same way scientists say that all matter is affected by thought. We understand that everything is affected by thought—and not just in the physical dimension. What the Zohar does is provide the tools to help raise consciousness. Water was never violent, but it became violent, since it was subjected to the sin of Adam and Eve and the negativity of humans. However, this does not mean that water has to remain this way.

The Zohar states that everything written about the Ark is a metaphor. Even if the Ark was really a boat, it could not have survived out there with all the rain, hail, and towering waves beating down on it. The Zohar states that restoring the Ark in Malchut is the way to create the Vessel. The only place to draw the Light is into the Vessel because the Light comes to Malchut only by way of the Sefira of Yesod. The reason we have negativity is because our world is Malchut—the dimension where Light and darkness are separate. Our world can only reflect Light—like the moon, it has no light of its own.

I have spoken with scientists and doctors who concentrate their efforts on removing negativity—such as cancer and other diseases—but we cannot completely remove negativity without removing the source. Similarly, when society wants to punish a murderer with the death penalty, thus removing him physically from the world, it still does not remove the negative consciousness that he injected into the world. The source of negativity must be removed, and only then will negative consciousness, such as violence, be eliminated.

Creating of the Ark Anew

What Noah did with the Ark was to draw the Light and abolish darkness. What we are doing through this reading is recreating the

Ark, which enables us to draw down the Lightforce and preserve the natural distribution of what God created in the universe. What we are seeking to achieve is the removal of darkness and violence—yet, unfortunately, this is only possible on Shabbat, which is what the Ark represents. With the reading of the portion of Noah, we create a Vessel, just as Noah did, to draw Light to control water and render it positive—as it was before the Sin of Adam. When Noah did this, the water went back to its original state and there was no more violence.

With this section, when we speak of 300 cubits, it concerns Chochmah, Binah, and Da'at. We are looking to remove evil intent with the Sefirot, by restoring the positive nature of water, a fundamental part of life. With this, we will affect violent behavior by affecting the cellular level of humankind. It is important to remember that our bodies are composed of nearly eighty percent water, so we have a direct and deep connection to the element.

Our purpose is to restore water to its original positive nature, and its role as a fundamental part of life. I have been asked if anyone can create the same water we have in the Centres, and I said potentially yes, they could—and one day soon that will happen. With this water we will affect everyone on the cellular level.

Consciousness and the Flood

Another fact that certainly deserves our attention is that there is so much emphasis placed on the land in this story. Why did the land have to suffer? What did the land do? All it did was serve the people. All the commentators ask in what way did the land corrupt itself? The land did not sin, but the people were evil, so we are told, and therefore the Earth and the land became corrupted.

The answer lies in the importance of consciousness, another great lesson we learn about the future technology that we can incorporate in our lives today. As much as we have discussed the way consciousness controls matter—which is verified by theoretical science—most of us do not fully comprehend it or certainly cannot maintain this consciousness continuously. There is so much information about mind over matter, but can we truly see its effects? Some of us have experienced phenomena beyond the normal range of physical reality. But are such events proof of mind over matter? Perhaps yes, perhaps no. Such occurrences happen so infrequently that there is no reason to believe that mind rules over matter.

All the biblical commentators agree that the evil consciousness of the Earth's inhabitants was literally transmitted to the soil. The Earth was indeed corrupted through the effect of mind over matter. The kabbalistic doctrine of mind over matter is an absolute, yet because there is no practical proof of this in applied physics, it is dismissed. Mind over matter exists as a theoretical truth, but on a very practical level science has not been able to effect change in the natural world through purely mental processes.

The truth of mind over matter is clearly portrayed in this section of the Bible. Why did the Earth have to undergo this kind of diminution and suffering? Today, we witness the way the Earth can be diminished in its capacity to grow trees or fruits. The branch of a tree that once produced 25 oranges, can be reduced to producing five. Everything in nature can be diminished. It is beautiful to see how an orange emerges from a flower. To see a fragile bud turn into an orange is to witness the Lightforce itself in action. It is an incredible sight.

The Dimensions of the Ark as Related to the Sefirot

What we learn in this portion concerns the existence of mind over matter. The Zohar explains that the dimensions of the Ark were not physical. There may or may not have been a ship—but this is not the reason for the dimensions being what they were. Logically speaking, such a little, box-like vessel could never survive the massive force and full extent of the Flood.

In a lengthy discourse, the Zohar explains that the dimensions of the Ark refer to the Sefirot. When we call upon the Sefirot, we realize that they have the ability to transfer the Lightforce of God, which is so powerful that it supersedes every physical form—all strength and all violence. The Sefirot are our protective shield, which is why we come back to this reading each year. It is certainly not to hear a story about Noah and the Ark as it is always told in children's books. We study this portion to discover how we can, again, year after year, reinstitute and reinforce our security shield—so that we are not vulnerable to the negativity that exists around us. This tale of Noah and the Ark is here to fulfill a need we all have—and a need that we will, unfortunately, always have until the force of Satan is finally removed from our midst.

We all have to contribute to the consciousness of mind over matter, and the more we contribute to this idea of understanding physical reality the more we will have control over it and its corresponding chaos. There is nothing that we cannot resolve if we put our minds and our consciousness to it.

We must begin to strengthen our imagination, so we are not confined to the prison Satan has created for us—the "box" in which most of us live.

The Origin of Water and the Lightforce of God

The Bible says that, at the time of the Flood, tremendous heat rose up from within the Earth. Today, we know of only a few volcanic geysers of varying temperatures that exist around the world—but at the time of the Flood the whole inner core of the Earth opened up. Neither cold water from the rain, nor the water in underground streams could overcome the heat of those geysers. Why was this?

Water is the only physical entity that existed on the first day of Creation. Where did it come from? The Bible does not say—all it says is that God hovered over the waters. Was water then in fact a creation at all? Why are we meant to assume it was just there? The Bible does not say that God created water. It says He created everything else on Earth, including humankind, but it does not mention whether God created water. Why is this?

I have only found one commentator who ever raised this question. Why is it so? It is because water is the Lightforce of God and, just as it is with the mystery of whether God created Himself, this is something beyond our understanding. Whence did it all originate—the people, the landscape around us, and the celestial bodies? We say they came from God but, as Rav Ashlag tells us, we will never understand while we are in this corporeal body. This is not because it is a secret but because there are boundaries our consciousness cannot cross. Rav Ashlag revealed to us that we can, however, comprehend the full constitution of the Lightforce of God. What is this Lightforce? As we have all learned from Rav Ashlag, it is the sharing capacity. God does not have within Himself a character of the Desire to Receive—even if for the sake of sharing. The Desire to Receive does not exist in the Lightforce.

Sharing is the quality of water in its purest state. When the Bible says *Yom Echad* or "One Day," "one" is like a seed—whatever can emerge from that seed is already intrinsically included in it. Water contains the physical aspect as we observe it, and also has the closest relationship to the Lightforce of God. In observing water, we can almost glimpse the nature of the Lightforce. The one element that exists throughout this entire world, yet is the least understood, is water. Everything is surrounded by water, everything is made up of water—and yet science knows precious little about it. Why is it that Moses could hit a stone and make water come forth from it? What is the origin of stone? Stone emerged from water—it came after water. Whence did the tree come? The seed. This is an indisputable rule of the universe, and there is no reason to deny that the seed contains everything. If not, whence did everything come?

The first day of Creation also contained water from the geysers and everything else. The evil inclination of the people of that day took all of the different aspects that were once *echad* or one"—which could only then operate in positivity—and out came geysers of steaming water, so hot that it literally melted flesh off bodies, brought fragmentation and destruction. Water today has the ability to be changed, just as it did at the time of the Flood. It is all about consciousness.

Why is it written that there was a flood of water? Does a flood by nature not have to be of water? With regard to Noah, the Zohar states "with the flood," meaning that the Angel of Death was present. This does not seem to provide an answer, however, and the Zohar is obscure here—but what it means to say is that the nature of the power of water is Chesed, which is solely positive and cannot kill. With the Flood, water became capable of causing death only because the spirit of the Angel of Death was present and unconcealed.

18 But I will establish My covenant with you, and you will enter the ark—you and your sons and your wife and your sons' wives with you. 19 And of every living thing of flesh, you are to bring two into the ark to keep them alive with you; they will be male and female. 20 Of birds of every kind, of cattle of every kind, and of every creeping creature of the earth of its kind, two of every sort will come to you to be kept alive. 21 And take every kind of food that is to be eaten, gather it and store it away as food for you and for them." 22 Thus did Noah accordingly all that God had commanded him, so he did.

Beresheet 7:1 And the Lord then said to Noah, "Come into the ark, you and your house, because I have found you righteous before Me in this generation. 2 Take with you in sevens of every kind of clean animal, a male and its female, and in twos of every kind of unclean animal, a male and its female. 3 Of every kind of bird also take in sevens, male and the female, to keep their seed alive upon the face of the earth.

Sevens and Twos

Rashi (Rabbi Shlomo Yitzchaki) famed commentator on the Bible, asks why Noah was told to "take with you in sevens of every kind of clean animal, a male and its female, and in twos of every kind of unclean animal, a male and its female"? Furthermore, there were no such things as kosher or non-kosher animals during Noah's time. The idea of kosher and non-kosher first came into existence at Mount Sinai. There were only seven precepts during the time of Noah. He was not commanded to adhere to the dietary laws at all. This troubled Rashi. Was this because, one day in the future, there would be a necessity for animals to be brought for sacrifice—so this was to ensure that there would be enough animals?

Contrary to popular belief, although Rashi is said to be the simplest commentator to understand on the Bible, anyone who delves into the text knows that Rashi is the most difficult commentator. In other words, it is only Kabbalah that makes things very simple. Rashi was selective about the words he used. What did Rashi want in explaining the fact that Noah was told "seven, a male and its female," and what did Rashi mean that, at a later date, at the time of the Holy Temple, there will be a necessity for bringing these animals for sacrifice? This does not sound logical—and it was never the intent of the Bible.

If we study Kabbalah, however, we immediately understand what the numbers *seven* and *two* mean—and therein lies the secret. This is what Rashi really means. The Zohar consistently says that every word in the Bible is a concealment, and is really there to teach us a hidden message. It is like a human being who has a body and a soul. The soul does not become expressed until there is a body to conceal it. If a person dies, the soul does not die but the soul is no longer permitted to express itself—because it requires the body to do this. Therefore, the body, which is the clothing, the cloak of the internal understanding of the Bible, had to be constructed the way it is. We cannot tell by looking at a person's face whether or not he or she is kind. There is no way to know what is going on internally—you have to delve deep below. Both the Zohar and the Ari say that, when the Bible says "seven, a male and its female," it is obviously referring to a structure of completeness. The reason Noah was told seven is because animals contain particular internal energies.

The reason a goat was sacrificed at the Holy Temple on Yom Kippur was because it contained a particular internal energy necessary to be released into the cosmos. The goat has a negative internal quality and, through slaughtering it, this energy was sweetened and released. There is a particular meditation by the Kohen (priest) that went into this performance of bringing animals for sacrifice. As he was slaughtering an animal, he knew that, through the release of this energy, the cosmos would now become full of a particular vibration necessary on that day. They brought only the kosher animals because all sacrifices were structures of energy. Rashi explained that the purpose of sacrificing these animals was to bring a different kind of metaphysical and physical environment into the universe, to create a balance therein.

Never should anyone think that the purpose of sacrifices was to appease God or, as the idol worshippers would say, to appease the gods. God does not need to be appeased. It would be a total aberration for any of us ever to assume that God needed this kind of pleasure. The moment we make such a statement, we are immediately denying what God is about—we are assuming God is like a father or mother or sister or son, whom we give a gift to please. This was not the idea behind the sacrifices. Rav Shimon said this could never be an intelligent interpretation of the Torah. It is a corruption, as Rav Shimon says. The Bible says *seven* because a structure of seven is a complete structure of energy designed to perform a particular function.

The reason *two* referred to the unclean animals is because the Bible is discussing Right and Left Columns, which are not balanced—because there is no Central Column. In the atom there is a proton, an electron, and the central neutron is the balancing agent. When there are only two forces—as there are in a lightbulb that has no filament—there is no circuit of energy. Therefore, the two are called unclean because the Hebrew word *tame* does not mean "unclean," it literally means, "lack of a circuit of energy," or even "short circuitry." The intrinsic characteristic of these animals is one of not having a balancing agent. Therefore, the dietary laws of not eating pig or other non-clean animals, are not because there is a religion that says which animals we can eat but rather it is to give us some support and knowledge concerning the internal energy forces that exist in animals so that we understand that when we ingest these kind of animals we are ingesting their internal energy force. We do not want to ingest a force that is not balanced and does not have the qualities of three, which is the Right, Left, and Central Column energy.

> **4 Seven days from now, I will cause it to rain upon the earth for forty days and forty nights, and every living thing that I have made I will destroy from off the face of the earth." 5 And Noah did accordingly all that the Lord commanded him. 6 And Noah was six hundred years old when the flood of waters was upon the earth. 7 And Noah and his sons and his wife and his son's wives entered the ark because of the waters of the flood. 8 Of clean beasts and unclean beasts, and of birds and of all creatures that creep upon the earth, 9 there went in two and two towards Noah and into the ark, the male and the female, as God had commanded Noah.**

The Ark, Water, and the Flawless Universe

The kabbalists have made a point of mentioning the number of verses we have in the portion of Noah, which is 153, making it one of the longest in the Bible. What is the meaning of 153? Where is the clue that can provide us with the understanding of this entire section? The name "Betzalel" adds up numerically to 153. Betzalel was the young man who constructed the Tabernacle in the wilderness.

Was Betzalel given this name because it adds up to 153 or was there another reason for it? As with the Holy Temple: Was it holy because God said to build it so He could live on Earth within it, or was there holiness in the Temple itself? But God does not dwell anywhere upon the Earth, does He? We state every day in our connections that, even without the Temple, God fills this entire universe. We are not referring to the Temple as a place in which God could dwell, but rather we are referring to the structure of the Temple. The physical manifestation itself provides us with the ability to connect to something as immaterial as the Lightforce of God. Humankind's consciousness cannot be limited to the physical world—and in this way the Ark provides a means to connect to the Lightforce. Despite the fact that the entire world was eliminated, this little Ark provided safety for those who were within it. There are many lessons to be learned in this portion.

When we look at the previous portion of Beresheet, we see that water was in a unified state on the first day of Creation, and was then separated on the Second Day. What was water separated from? Water was separated from Binah, the Flawless Universe—the dimension we strive to connect to—to enable us to avoid the chaos that surrounds us each and every day in the realm of Malchut, the realm where chaos manifests. It is our endeavor to attempt to bridge these two universes—Malchut, the chaotic universe, the one with which we are familiar and Binah, the Flawless Universe. How do we achieve this unification?

On Day One of Creation, this physical world of Malchut and the Flawless Universe already existed. When the Temple existed, it was our opportunity to connect to the Lightforce of God—which is the Flawless Universe—and thereby influence the physical world of humankind. The physical world and humanity's chaotic activity could not then exert its influence of chaos over the Flawless Universe. The separation that existed was only in a potential state. It is left to humankind to determine ultimately what is to be done with chaos.

The Destructive Force of the Flood and God's Anger

In this section, we have a description of the Deluge, and it becomes clear that, not only did the land become polluted because of negative human activity, but there was also a separation from the waters that were in a potential state. In other words, this action made manifest what was in a potential state. Such an outcome can only occur due to human consciousness. On every possible occasion, I will repeat the following point a thousand times, and only then will we perhaps begin to recognize its truth. The expressions "God was angry," "God punishes," "because of God's wrath, He brought the flood," do not deviate in any way from anything else that is said in Bible. In other words, from a strictly literal level of the Bible, you could say that, because of humanity's negativity, God brought His wrath down upon them. But the Zohar says there is nothing in the universe besides the beneficent nature of the Lightforce of God.

Although every movement takes place by the Lightforce of God, humanity's negative activity can create chaos even out of the Lightforce's perfection. It is the same way an electrical current can produce clear light to illuminate our lives—yet it also has the potential to create a fire or a lethal shock. It is not the electricity's intent to create a fire—rather it is our ineptitude that leads to the abuse or misuse of the current that can result in a fire or shock. In the same way, the Deluge did not begin with the anger of God—it was the result of human activity. This is the one lesson we should learn regarding any form of chaos that comes upon us. When we are angry at God—when we say, "Lord, why did You do this to me?"—we should listen to the Zohar's interpretation that it was not God's intention to cause any harm. Our misfortunes are not due to God's anger.

The Upper and Lower Waters

In the portion of Noah, human negativity polluted the Earth's waters. Water is what makes up 70 to 80 percent of this world, and our bodily cells contain 80 percent water. Water essentially has the power of unity. It creates a balance, and that is why water existed on *Yom Echad*, the first day of Creation, the day of Unity. It was humankind who took water and polluted it, and thus caused it to lose its ability to create balance. If we were somehow able to remove all impurities in our water, so that there was no semblance of pollution left within it, we could live forever. Noah lived through the Flood because he did not pollute the water—he was in possession of the water of *Yom Echad*, the first day of Creation. This is why we are given this reading, not to listen to a tale we have heard countless times before but to tap into the power of water.

Water has the ability to help us maintain balance in our lives, provided we do not separate the Upper and Lower Waters from one another, the Malchut from Binah, which would be separating the physical manifestation, which has the potential of human negativity, from the Flawless Universe. It is left to us either to pollute or to make every effort to join the Flawless Universe of Binah. This is the central teaching in this reading.

10 And it came to pass after seven days; the waters of the flood were upon the earth. 11 In the six-hundredth year of Noah's life, on the seventeenth day of the second month—on that day all the fountains (springs) of the great deep burst forth, and the floodgates of the heavens were opened. 12 And rain fell upon the earth forty days and forty nights. 13 On that same day Noah and Shem, and Ham and Japheth, the sons of Noah and Noah's wife and the three wives of his sons with them, entered the ark. 14 They and every beast according to its kind, all the cattle according to their kinds, every creature that creeps upon the ground according to its kind and every fowl according to its kind, every bird of every sort. 15 They went towards Noah into the ark, two and two of all flesh wherein there is the breath of life. 16 And they went in, male and female of all flesh, as God had commanded Noah; and the Lord shut him in.

Evil Eye and the Ark

Rav Isaac Luria (the Ari) asked why Noah was only saved by means of an Ark. Was there no other way for God to save him? Beresheet 7:18 says: "And the waters prevailed and increased greatly upon the Earth and the Ark went upon the face of the waters, and the waters prevailed exceedingly high." What kind of water was this? The Zohar says that everything opened up from the Heavens, and also from below in the earth. This was not the kind of situation in which an ark could survive. The Zohar says the dimension of the Ark was not something physical—it had to do with making use of energy-forces. The Ark was a security shield—nothing less, nothing more.

Noah was advised by God how to structure something that the violence of nature could not overcome—an energy shield that would withstand everything. But why did he need the physical box to do this? The Zohar informs us that Noah was told to create a box because a person is never to reveal themselves physically when there are negative energy-forces around. The Zohar explains that, because of the aspect of *ayin hara* or "evil eye," it was not sufficient for Noah to create only a metaphysical security shield—it was necessary that there be a physical Ark as well.

It says in the Zohar there are three things that are fixed when we are born: how many children we will have, how long we will live, and how much wealth we will accumulate. This is so to make everyone fulfilled. The world was not created for the benefit of suffering. It was not the objective of God to create a world of misery—so why is misery so prevalent for us?

Both the Zohar and the Talmud say most people die before their time because of the evil eye. There are people who have no way of knowing how to control their longevity. Most premature deaths are due to this evil eye. Why is there a prevalence of disease in one individual, and not in another? It is not a question of luck. Everyone has cancer cells, and everyone is vulnerable, so why is one person more vulnerable than another? The answer is that, if a person's security shield has been penetrated by evil eye, then there is a breakdown of the immune system, which is innately structured in every human being at birth.

Evil eye comes in many forms. For instance, at a cemetery, the Angel of Death is present. This is his home, and thus, by letting down their security shields, people can open themselves up to attack by him in a cemetery. We, and not something out there, are the initiators of this vulnerability. It is not a matter of luck. Therefore, to physically conceal and create a security shield that would protect from exposure to evil eye, the Zohar says it was necessary for Noah to create the physical Ark. Noah built an energy-field around himself.

We all have an aura around us that expresses our internal energy. The reason we are able to feel others is because their energy-fields convey who they really are. This is why we intrinsically feel more comfortable with certain people, and uncomfortable with others—sometimes even without speaking one word to them. According to the Zohar, our energy-field extends to an area of 88 inches. Anyone entering within these 88 inches can feel us. The people around us will feel if we are a negative or positive person, even though we have never transmitted any form of negativity or positivity. It has nothing to do with a physical action. Someone who may not even know us is able to feel who we really are. The more spiritual and attuned we are, the more we can immediately spot these things all around us.

Noah created the physical Ark to prevent the physical penetration of his security shield by the evil force, the destroyer—Satan. The waters of the flood could not penetrate Noah's metaphysical security shield, but the only thing that can keep away the eyes of demons is a physical security shield—this is why it was necessary for Noah to create a physical Ark.

17 And the flood was forty days upon the earth, and as the waters increased they lifted the ark high above the earth. 18 The waters prevailed and increased greatly upon the earth, and the ark floated upon the face of the waters. 19 And the waters prevailed exceedingly upon the earth, and all the high hills that were under the entire heaven were covered. 20 Fifteen cubits upward did the waters prevail; and the mountains were covered. 21 And all flesh that moved upon the earth died—birds, cattle, beasts, all the creatures that creep over the earth, and every man, 22 all in whose nostrils was the breath of life, all that was on dry land died. 23 Every living thing on the face of the earth was destroyed; both man and cattle, and the creeping things, and the birds of the heaven were wiped from the earth; only Noah remained alive, and those that were with him in the ark. 24 And the waters prevailed upon the earth for a hundred and fifty days.

The Generation of the Flood

Why was the world destroyed specifically by water? It could have been by an earthquake or something else. According to the Zohar, in *Gehenom* or Hell, there are six months of fire and six months of water. The Flood was also like this, comprising both fire and water.

The people of the generation of the Flood took water, which is Chesed, and is the closest in essence to the Light, and they turned it into something negative.

Beresheet 8:1 And God remembered Noah and every living thing, and all the cattle that were with him in the ark, and God made a wind to pass over the earth, and the waters assuaged. 2 The fountains also of the deep and the windows of heaven were stopped, and the rain from heaven was restrained. 3 And the waters receded steadily from off the earth. At the end of the hundred and fifty days, the waters were abated. 4 And on the seventeenth day of the seventh month, the ark came to rest on the mountains of Ararat. 5 And the waters decreased continually until the tenth month, and on the first day of the tenth month the tops of the mountains became visible. 6 And it came to pass at the end of forty days that Noah opened the window he had made in the ark, 7 and he sent out a raven, which went forth flying back and forth until the water had dried up from off the earth. 8 Then he sent out a dove to see if the water had dried up from the surface of the earth. 9 But the dove could find no rest for the sole of her foot because there was water over all the surface of the earth; so she returned to Noah in the ark. He reached out his hand and took the dove and brought it back to him in the ark. 10 And he stayed yet another seven days and again sent out the dove from the ark. 11 And the dove returned to him in the evening, and lo, there was a freshly plucked olive leaf in its beak. So Noah knew that the waters had receded from off the earth. 12 And he waited yet another seven days and sent the dove out again, but this time it did not return to him. 13 By the first day of the first month of Noah's six hundredth and first year, the waters had dried up from off the face of the earth; and Noah removed the covering from the ark and saw that the face of the ground was dry. 14 And in the second month, on the twenty-seventh day of the month, the earth was completely dry. 15 And God spoke to Noah saying, 16 "Go forth from the ark, you and your wife and your sons and your son's wives with you; 17 Bring out every kind of living thing that is of all flesh that is with you—the birds, the cattle, and all the creatures that creep along the ground—so that they may breed abundantly on the earth and be fruitful and multiply on the earth." 18 And Noah came out, together with his sons and his wife and his sons' wives, 19 every beast, every creeping thing and every bird—everything that moves on the earth—came out of the ark, one kind after another.

The Ark as Protection from Chaos

Noah was a righteous person (a *tzadik*), and we know that a *tzadik* is the connection to Yesod, the realm above the physical chaotic existence—above Malchut. Noah survived because either he had left this physical level or because he had combined the two worlds and thus became one with their union. Noah did not survive because of the physical dimensions of the structure of the boat—the dimensions of which, in truth, indicate different elements of Sefirot—he survived because he created a security shield that acted as protection from the devastation that ensued.

The Lightforce travels through the Sefirot in a non-physical manner, and the physical structure of the Ark was an instrument for the Sefirot to be combined to create a security shield in the physical dimension.

Reading the Bible is a physical action, and thereby we are also provided with a security shield. Shabbat is only once a week but with it we can preserve every other week that lies before us. What we are capturing with this reading is a security shield, so that we will not be affected by what is currently going on in the world around us.

As we have discussed previously, the word *teiva* actually means either "box" or "word." What is being described here is how we can "box" ourselves in with a protection shield—there is no other way to survive. We could have a bodyguard outside our homes, and think we are safe but even if we do not leave our room ever, we still cannot prevent a heart attack. There is a lot that can go on inside that "box" of ours—we cannot escape a life lived with chaos.

Noah and Commitment

The Zohar says that a righteous person is someone who has achieved the level of consciousness known as the Sefira of Yesod. When a person connects to this realm, death no longer exists for them. The Zohar asks how it is, since Noah was a *tzadik*, that he could not nullify death in the world and prevent the Deluge from taking place. The Zohar then answers that the people of Noah's generation did not believe Noah when he warned them that a flood was coming and said he wanted to teach them how to protect themselves. Noah believed it and, because he was a *tzadik*, he had the energy-intelligence level to save the whole world. But like most people today, the people then were full of ego and felt that they were in control of their destiny. They also did not believe that it was possible to create a security shield around themselves.

Why is this so important? The Zohar says that, when we want something to work for us, it requires total commitment. If a person is not totally committed to do whatever they want to do, they will never succeed at it. Total commitment means more than just thinking that something is a good idea and so we will do it. The word for "commitment" in Hebrew is *hitchayvut*, which comes from the word *chayav*, meaning "a connection." There is a necessity for total commitment in everything we do because we cannot have a fragmented life or career—there must be an understanding from the beginning to the end of every endeavor. Successful people are always totally committed to whatever they are doing. People who do things because they have to, or because there is no alternative, curtail the complete flow of energy that the cosmos wants to interject into their undertakings, thus limiting this energy, making it slow and weak.

At the time of the Flood, the people did not die because God wanted to destroy them, even if they deserved to be destroyed. They did not believe Noah—there was no total commitment—and because of this they could not be saved.

Also in this portion is the incident of the Tower of Babel. People of the highest intelligence desired to build a skyscraper to reach the Heavens. Today, we have difficulty building something 140 storeys high, even with all of the recent advancements in technology and science. But these people were already reaching the sky. Yet their purpose was evil, and the Zohar says that these people could not be destroyed because they were totally committed to each other.

When we are totally committed, we have a complete flow of energy. If we do something halfheartedly, if there is no total commitment, it is not going to work because without a total commitment, as the Zohar says, it is impossible to achieve anything.

20 And Noah built an altar to the Lord and took of every clean beast and every clean bird and offered burnt offerings on it. 21 And the Lord smelled a sweet savor and the Lord said in his heart: "I will not again curse the ground for man's sake, for the inclination of his heart is evil from his youth: never again will I smite every living thing, as I have done. 22 While the earth remains, seedtime and harvest, and cold and heat, summer and winter, and day and night shall not cease."

Beresheet 9:1 And God blessed Noah and his sons, saying to them, "Be fruitful and multiply and replenish the earth. 2 And the fear and dread of you will fall upon every beast of the earth and every bird of the air, upon every creature that creeps along the ground, and upon all the fish of the sea; they are given into your hands. 3 Every moving thing that lives will be meat for you. Just as I gave you the green herbs, I now give you everything. 4 But flesh with the life thereof, which is the blood thereof, you shall not eat. 5 And surely your blood of your lives will I require, at the hand of every beast will I require it, and at the hand of man; at the hand of every man's brother will I require the life of man. 6 Whosoever sheds the blood of man, by man shall his blood be shed; for in the image of God made He man. 7 And you be fruitful and multiply; bring forth abundantly in the earth and multiply upon it." 8 And God spoke to Noah and to his sons with him saying: 9 "Behold, I establish My covenant with you and with your seed after you; 10 and with every living creature that is with you—the birds, the cattle, and all the wild beasts of the earth with you, from all that go out of the ark to every beast on earth. 11 And I will establish My covenant with you: Never again will all flesh be cut off by the waters of a flood; never again will there be a flood to destroy the earth. 12 And God said, "This is the sign of a covenant which I make between Me and you and every living creature that is with you, for perpetual generations: 13 I do set my bow in the cloud, and it will be a sign of a covenant between Me and the earth. 14 And it shall come to pass when I bring a cloud over the earth, that the bow shall be seen in the cloud; 15 and I will remember My covenant which is between Me and you and every living creature of all flesh, and the waters shall no more become a flood to destroy all flesh. 16 And the bow shall be in the cloud; and I will look upon it and remember the everlasting covenant between God and every living creature of all flesh that is upon the earth." 17 And God said to Noah, "This is the sign of the covenant I have established between Me and all flesh that is upon the earth."

The Rainbow: God's Covenant with Noah

The water receded and Noah was told to go out of the Ark, and God said that He would establish a covenant with him. God assured Noah another deluge would not be brought about and, on seeing this rainbow, God would remember His promise—it would be a sign that He would not again destroy civilization. This is so absurd that it barely deserves a comment—as if God could have a short memory.

Why was it not enough for the Creator to say He would not bring another flood? Why did He also need the sign of a rainbow to indicate that there would not be any more disasters or floods? What about the storms and hurricanes that have been destroying cities throughout history since the time of Noah? The answer is that it was to help people. To be in oneness was the only spiritual work during the generation of the Flood. Today, the work is in achieving restriction—the purpose of the Central Column. The rainbow's purpose was to signify that, with the power of resistance, which is expressed by three colors—green, white, and red—it would be possible to avert destruction and annihilation. The rainbow is a symbol for how to save the whole world.

The rainbow was not created so that God would not forget. Through it, God spoke and said that the Lightforce can control every physical aspect of the universe. However, because of Bread of Shame, it can only respond according to the rules of Creation. Without exercising restriction over our evil inclination, without developing a sharing nature, mind over matter is useless.

The Zohar says that the rainbow is a message. The three colors represent the balance of receiving and sharing. We learn in Kabbalah to apply these principles by the virtue of restriction. White is the Right Column energy of sharing, Red is the Left

Column energy of receiving, and Green is the Central Column energy of restricting. In this way we can control every aspect of Creation—including water. What God said through the rainbow is that, if people are in this balanced position, then there would be no reason for the evil eye. What do people achieve with evil eye? Not only do they not get what they want, they lose what they already possess. This is so contrary to the way the world was originally established, on the first day of Creation.

18 And the sons of Noah that went out of the ark were Shem, and Ham, and Japheth; and Ham is the father of Canaan. 19 These were the three sons of Noah, and from them the whole world was overspread. 20 And Noah began to be a husbandman and planted a vineyard. 21 And he drank of the wine, and became drunk and he was uncovered inside his tent. 22 And Ham, the father of Canaan, saw his father's nakedness and told his two brothers outside. 23 And Shem and Japheth took a garment and laid it across their shoulders; then they walked in backward and covered their father's nakedness; and their faces were turned away, and they did not see their father's nakedness. 24 And Noah awoke from his wine and knew what his youngest son had done to him, 25 and he said, "Cursed be Canaan; a servant of servants shall he be to his brothers." 26 And he said, "Blessed be the Lord, the God of Shem; and Canaan shall be his servant. 27 God shall enlarge Japheth; and he shall live in the tents of Shem, and Canaan shall be his servant." 28 And Noah lived 350 years after the flood. 29 All the days of Noah were 950 years, and he died.

Beresheet 10:1 Now these are the generations of the sons of Noah: Shem, Ham, and Japheth, who themselves had sons after the flood. 2 The sons of Japheth: Gomer, and Magog, and Madai, and Javan, and Tubal, and Meshech, and Tiras. 3 And the sons of Gomer: Ashkenaz, and Riphath, and Togarmah. 4 And the sons of Javan: Elishah, and Tarshish, the Kitites, and the Rodanites, 5 By these were the Gentiles spread out into their lands, each with their own language, by their families within their nations. 6 And the sons of Ham: Cush, Mizra'im, and Put, and Canaan. 7 And the sons of Cush: Seba, Havilah, and Sabtah, and Ra'amah and Sabteca, and the sons of Ra'amah: Sheba and Dedan. 8 And Cush was the father of Nimrod, who grew to be a mighty one on the earth. 9 He was a mighty hunter before the Lord; wherefore it is said, "Even as Nimrod, the mighty hunter before the Lord." 10 And the beginning of his kingdom was Babylon, and Erech, and Akkad, and Calneh, in the land of Shinar, 11 Out of that land went forth Asshur, who built Nineveh, and the city Rehoboth, and Calah, 12 and Resen, which is between Nineveh and Calah; that is the great city. 13 And Mizra'im became the father of the Ludites, Anamites, Lehabites, Naphtuhites, 14 and Pathrusites, Casluhites (from whom the Philistines came), and Caphtorites. 15 And Canaan was the father of Sidon, his firstborn, and the Hittites, 16 Jebusites, Amorites, Girgashites, 17 Hivites, Arkites, Sinites, 18 Arvadites, Zemarites, and Hamathites; the families of the the Canaanite spread abroad. 19 And the border of the Canaanites was from Sidon, toward Gerar, up to Gaza, and then toward Sodom, Gomorrah, and Admah, and Zebo'im, even as far as Lasha. 20 These are the sons of Ham by their families and by their languages, in their countries and in their nations. 21 Unto Shem, the father of all the children of Eber and whose older brother was Japheth, even to him children were born. 22 The children of Shem: Elam, and Asshur, and Arphaxad, and Lud, and Aram. 23 And the children of Aram: Uz, and Hul, and Gether, and Mash. 24 And Arphaxad was the father of Shelah, and Shelah was the father of Eber. 25 And two sons were born to Eber: One was named Peleg, because in his days the earth was divided; his brother's name was Joktan. 26 And Joktan was the father of Almodad, and Sheleph, and Hazar-Maveth, and Jerah, 27 And Hadoram, and Uzal, and Diklah, 28 and Obal, and Abimael, and Sheba, 29 and Ophir, and Havilah and Jobab: all these were the sons of Joktan. 30 And their dwelling was from Mesha toward Sephar, a mount of the east. 31 These are the sons of Shem by their families and their languages, in their lands and in their nations. 32 These are the families of the sons of Noah, after their generations, in their nations; and by these were the nations divided over the earth after the flood.

Beresheet 11:1 And the whole world had one language and one speech. 2 And it came to pass, as they journeyed from the east that they found a plain in the land of Shinar and they settled there. 3 And they said to each other, "Come, let's make bricks and bake them thoroughly." They had brick instead of

stone, and slime for mortar. 4 And they said, "Come, let us build a city, and a tower that reaches to heaven, and let us make ourselves a name lest we are scattered upon the face of the whole earth." 5 And the Lord came down to see the city and the tower that the children of men were building. 6 And the Lord said, "Behold the people are one and they all have one language that they have begun to do, and now nothing will restrain them from what they plan to do. 7 Come, let Us go down and confuse their language so that they will not understand one another's speech." 8 So the Lord scattered them abroad from there over the face of all the earth, and they stopped building the city. 9 That is why it was called Babel—because there the Lord confused the language of the whole world, and from there the Lord scattered them abroad over the face of all the earth.

The Tower of Babel and the Unifying Quality of Hebrew

Concerning the Tower of Babel, why was there nothing the Creator could do to stop the people? The answer is that they had unity and accord, and they also had the 72 Names of God. For example, with the *Mem, Hei, Shin* we can actualize the power of healing that exists in the world. Similarly, each of the 72 Names of God comprises the entirety of the Lightforce of God, and one who connects to them is protected from the negativity and evil in the world—nothing can harm them. This is why the Kabbalah Centres' War Room walls are covered with the 72 Names of God—and the Hebrew letters connect us to the Light. What the Creator did to the people

of Babel was simply to confound their language, causing them
to scatter.

What would happen if someone today were to find the 72 Names of
God in the Zohar, which could render them invincible? The reality
is that if this person is not in oneness and in the consciousness of
"love your neighbor," then the Names would simply not work for
them. If someone has any hatred for another person or any anger
within them, then they lack the most necessary quality. As soon
as they separate from others, the force of divisiveness arises within
them. When it is written that the Creator dispersed the people of
Babel, it means divisiveness was within them—and this is why they
could be physically next to each other without communicating.

The people intended to build a skyscraper, an edifice that was
already three thousand storeys high—it was beyond any concept
of structural logic. It was impossible. They almost succeeded too
because their abilities were so advanced that they could do what
would be thought impossible. However, their intentions were evil.

Beresheet 11:6 is a short biblical verse that has a long Zoharic
explanation. This verse was never mentioned during my post-
rabbinical studies, nor was it mentioned throughout all my years
of study in the Yeshiva. During the period described in this biblical
portion, there was only one language. What was that language? The
Bible does not say. How did God thwart the people's evil intentions?
He created other languages, so they could not communicate with
each other—and this brought down the Tower of Babel.

The Zohar says that, before this incident of the Tower of Babel,
there was only one language—Hebrew—and that this language
brought about a unity, which is scarcely conceivable today. The
Hebrew letters kept the entire world together, and they also
controlled disease, along with all physical matter. This language is a

138

protection for the entire world, and such an understanding will one day return. There was only one nation, and then they were divided. I could give a thousand lectures and elicit a thousand questions on this one section. The entire world can be restored to a level of existence without chaos. We may not be able to do this for the entire world, but at least, through the wisdom of this reading, we can do it for ourselves today.

The Bible says that the whole planet had one language, and everything was then unified. What is the relationship between this language and unification? The longer it takes us to dispel the myth about the Hebrew language—about the *Alef Bet*—only belonging to those in Israel, the longer chaos will remain. I have studied Hebrew all my life—however, I could read it but I could not speak it. Only when I lived in Israel did I begin to speak it. There is a difference between reading and speaking this language. Only because of the Zohar are we aware of the language the people of Babel spoke. Only the Zohar provides us with the information that it was the *Alef Bet*.

This verse is only seven Hebrew words in length, yet it tells us everything there is to know about what we have been discussing up until this point. We want technology that will improve our lives—and all the wonders we seek can be accomplished through this one language. This one language removes the limitations of time, space, and motion—the nature of which consists of fragmentation, danger, and violence. Peace and unity can be achieved through this one language, and the technology developed from it.

The compendium of the Zohar, together with the *Sefer Yetzirah* ("Book of Formation"), and all the teachings of Kabbalah—solely by virtue of the language in which it is written—bring in an energy that cannot be described in words.

Each and every single one of us can bring this consciousness to others. If we do not, they will not be taught, and the struggle will be more difficult. This is the technology. One language will create unity and remove the fragmentation of time, space, and motion—or friction and gravity, which are also fragmentation and separation. This language does not belong to the Jews—it is a universal language. In a state of union, everyone will not become like everyone else—there is simply the removal of separation and pain.

10 These are the generations of Shem. Shem was one hundred years old, and he became the father of Arphaxad, two years after the flood. 11 And after Shem became the father of Arphaxad, he lived five hundred years and had other sons and daughters. 12 And Arphaxad lived thirty-five years, and he became the father of Shelah. 13 And Arphaxad lived four hundred and three years after he became the father of Shelah, and had other sons and daughters. 14 And Shelah lived thirty years, and he became the father of Eber. 15 And Shelah lived four hundred and three years after he became the father of Eber, and had other sons and daughters. 16 And Eber lived thirty-four years, and he became the father of Peleg. 17 And Eber lived four hundred and thirty years after he became the father of Peleg, and had other sons and daughters. 18 And Peleg lived thirty years, and he became the father of Reu. 19 And Peleg lived two hundred and nine years after he became the father of Reu, and had other sons and daughters. 20 And Reu lived thirty-two years, and he became the father of Serug. 21 And Reu lived two hundred and seven years after he became the father of Serug, and had other sons and daughters. 22 And Serug lived thirty years, and he became the father of Nahor. 23 And Serug lived two hundred years after he became the father of Nahor, and had other sons and daughters. 24 And Nahor lived twenty-nine years, and he became the father of Terah. 25 And Nahor

lived one hundred and nineteen years after he became the father of Terah, and had other sons and daughters. 26 And Terah lived seventy years, and he became the father of Abram, Nahor, and Haran. 27 Now these are the generations of Terah. Terah became the father of Abram, Nahor, and Haran. And Haran became the father of Lot. 28 And Haran died before his father in the land of his birth, in Ur of the Chaldees. 29 And Abram and Nahor both married. The name of Abram's wife was Sarai, and the name of Nahor's wife was Milcah; the daughter of Haran, the father of Milcah and the father of Iscah. 30 But Sarai was barren; she had no child. 31 And Terah took his son Abram, and his grandson Lot, son of Haran, and Sarai, his daughter-in-law, his son Abram's wife, and together they left Ur of the Chaldeans to go to the land of Canaan. But when they came to Haran, they settled there. 32 And Terah lived two hundred and five years, and Terah died in Haran.

Scorpio, the Flood, Taurus, and the Holy Temple

The portion of Noah will always be read on Shabbat in the Hebrew month of Cheshvan or Scorpio. According to all commentators on the Bible, the month of Scorpio is a very negative month, in fact it is known as Mar Cheshvan or "Bitter Cheshvan." Why is the month of Scorpio called "bitter"? We do not refer to the Hebrew month of Av (Leo), the month when the Holy Temple was destroyed, as "bitter." It is called Menachem Av, meaning "consolation." The destruction of the Temple was not necessarily evil but rather it was a cleansing process—and these take place throughout history.

From a kabbalistic point of view, we do not consider anything as an act of nature, meaning without a cause. In the month of Scorpio, there was another cleansing of everything that took place. To understand why the month of Scorpio is called "bitter," let us to turn to 1 Kings 6:37-38, concerning the building of the Holy Temple in Jerusalem:

> "The foundation of the Temple of the Lord was laid in the fourth year, in the month of *Ziv*. In the eleventh year in the month of Bul, the eighth month, the Temple was finished in all its details according to its specifications. He had spent seven years building it."

Is this a book telling us a little history? No. Rav Shimon said that if anyone treats the books of the Bible and the Prophets as stories, they are a fool, and will never come to the realization of the Bible's objective in setting down these stories and parables. The only reason for the biblical recording of history was to provide us with a form of energy. It was not to provide us with information—nor was it to provide us with a religion. It was to set down a path by which we would be able to receive the energy to take better control of our own lives.

The Zohar, and many other commentators refer to the month of Taurus (Iyar) as the month of *Ziv*. Why did King Solomon choose the month of *Ziv* or Taurus to begin his construction of the Temple? Was there no other month from which to choose? The Zohar and other commentaries explain that Solomon was a wise man, and when he chose the month of Taurus to begin the construction of the Temple, he had a reason. King Solomon's decision was in step with the cosmos. The Holy Temple was a satellite for all the awesome power of the cosmos to prevail over the whole world. The world was at total peace during the time that the Temple existed. There were no wars, there was no conflict; there was total serenity and peace. King Solomon did not indiscriminately choose this month. He knew that, for the Temple to physically serve the purpose of bringing Light and energy to the world, it was necessary for him to begin construction in the month of *Ziv*. The word *Ziv* means "flowing," a flowing of Light, of energy. Rav Shimon chose to leave this world in the month of Taurus for the same reason that King Solomon chose this month to begin the construction of the Temple.

We are told that the month of Taurus is a high-powered month of energy, and yet the month of Taurus is also a month of holocaust—this is the month in which a plague took the lives of 24,000 students of Rabbi Akiva. According to the sages, the month of Taurus is a month in which we refrain from festivities and from beginning new ventures, like opening a business, purchasing property, and getting married. This is true for the month as a whole, with the exception of one day, the 33rd day of Taurus—the day Rav Shimon chose to leave this world. On the 33rd day of Taurus, people get married, begin new ventures, sign contracts, and there is much festivity.

King Solomon completed the structure of the Holy Temple in the month of *Bul*, which is the eighth month of the year, the month of Scorpio. Did this mean that they, like contractors, worked to meet a certain deadline or schedule? Obviously, this was not the case with King Solomon—so why did he choose the month that delivered the total destruction of the entire world to complete the Temple?

Rav Isaac Luria (the Ari) asks why the prophet did not call these two months by their names—Iyar (Taurus) and Cheshvan (Scorpio)—instead of *Ziv* and *Bul*, respectfully—to indicate the months of the beginning and completion of the building of the Temple? When we study the Zohar or the Writings of the Ari, it is not simply a learning session to gather more information, but rather it is an energy-session to connect with the forces that are available in these two months.

The Zohar also says that the first day of the lunar month of Cheshvan or Scorpio, the month of *Bul*, contains the most powerful energy-intelligence of the year. It is the most powerful and positive day of the year—and by connecting with this day we receive that energy. There is no better day to start new things. Yet this seems to conflict with what we mentioned earlier, that Scorpio is known as Mar Cheshvan, a month of bitterness, a month of deluge, of flood.

Why did God choose Mar Cheshvan to bring the Flood, and why are there no holidays in the month of Scorpio? Were there no holidays because there was a flood in this month? No. At the Kabbalah Centres, we say that it is always the other way around—the cause brings on an effect. The Hebrew word for holiday, *chag*, is a code word for "balanced energy." When the Bible describes certain holidays, it is only informing us about what energy is available in the cosmos at that time. In other words, holidays, like Rosh Hashanah, Shavuot, Pesach and so on, are forms of energy that appear at particular times in the year. They do not mean a day of celebration, in terms of getting together or having a family meal. The holidays are meant for one specific purpose, which is to define for us what is going on in the cosmos. The reason that Cheshvan does not have holidays is not because of the Flood, it is because this is the month of an unequal balance of positivity. When we are overly good to our children, do they appreciate the good we keep doing for them? Not always. While the energy of Cheshvan is a very powerful force for good, everyone understands that overly-good is not good.

Most of us are affected by robotic-consciousness. Our ego allows us to think that we are really in control of our life. But who is really in control of their own destiny? Is it luck when someone missed being involved in an accident on the highway? Or is it unlucky if a drunken driver hits another car, even when that car's driver proceeds carefully and safely? Most of us do not have control over our lives, and this is the most difficult part of teaching Kabbalah. Because of the ego, no human being would like to admit that decisions are made for them. *What do you mean I do not decide? I am a thinking human being, I have intelligence…* and so on. But we do not decide. Both Kabbalah and theoretical physics say we are governed, influenced by things beyond our control. Quantum theory suggests that someone in one part of the world can create an energy with their actions that can influence a person on the other side of the world. Can we understand this logic? The cosmos leads our lives for us, if we permit the cosmos to lead our lives. There is no such thing as lucky or unlucky, according to the Bible.

The Flood happened in Scorpio because this is the month when ordinary water becomes a flood. We fear a flood, and yet water is the source of existence—most of the human body is made up of water. We need water to live, and without it, there is no life. So we can immediately notice that there is a benefit to water, and at the same time see that for every good and positive trait there is an equal and opposite negative and evil quality—like everything in this world. What or who determines how things behave? What determines whether water will act as a reservoir for sustaining life or will, instead, suddenly turn into a deluge? What determines the fact that someone drowns? Rav Shimon says that if we follow our robotic-consciousness, and are governed by the cosmos, we must know that Scorpio will be a bitter month.

We know that circuitry requires the principle of a positive and negative pole. Energy flows through the positive pole and the negative pole draws this current. It requires the positive pole to bring it into fruition. It is the positivity that makes Light-energy flow. Water has the internal energy-intelligence of positivity. Yes, water has consciousness because water contains atoms, which are intelligences. Water has the energy-intelligence of Desire to Share. Everything in our environment has energy-intelligence, and consequently it influences us. This is why, when we move into a new home, it is important to inquire who lived there before, and what took place there because the very walls will influence us. This phenomenon is known to theoretical physics—and it is known in Kabbalah. What determines why we live in a particular town? Is it because we like the area or is it because this is where the people we want to associate with live? No, there is something else driving that reality—there is very little we decide for ourselves. However, this does not mean we cannot decide anything.

At the end of the month of Tishrei (Libra), the month preceding Scorpio, with the holiday of Sukkot, there is an abundance of Chesed, the Right Column positive energy of water. This, at least, answers our question about why King Solomon completed the Temple in this month.

Scorpio is called the month of *Bul*, which in Hebrew means "stamp." But according to interpretation of this word in the Prophets, it means *bilbul* or "a mixing-up of things." *Bilbul* comes from the words *levalvel* and naval, which mean "decaying" or "things breaking down." Water has the power to break down anything—even a rock. Given sufficient time, there is nothing that can withstand water. This is why the *mabul* caused the breaking down of all of humankind. Scorpio is the month that has the greatest potential for disintegration.

There is a law in the Talmud that says, if we are in the middle of the *Amida*—the most important prayer that we recite during the day—and a king should pass by and extend his hand in greeting, we are not permitted to respond. However, if a scorpion should cross our path, we are permitted to interrupt our prayer and kill it. What about a snake or a grizzly bear? The answer is no. Some of the commentators explain that the reason for killing a scorpion is because it is blind, and kills without reason—to the extent that it even kills itself. It is the only creature that will kill itself. Like a snake, a scorpion has venom, but a snake will never kill itself. The Zohar says that a snake will never attack an individual unless it has been directed from Above to fulfill a particular objective. A scorpion has no objectives, and will thus even kill itself.

What brought about this characteristic in a scorpion? To truly understand the energy available in the month of Scorpio, we examine the Hebrew word for scorpion, *akrav*. We have previously discussed the power of the Hebrew *Alef Bet*, which the Zohar says is the only way that we can control the entire cosmos, and our own destiny. The four letters that make up the word akrav are *Ayin, Kuf, Resh,* and *Bet*. The two outside letters of this name, *Ayin* and *Bet*, numerically add up to 72, meaning the 72 Names of God that we make use of for a multitude of things—protection, healing, success, and so forth. Rav Shimon says we can be masters of our own destiny, and that the 72 Names of God, which are mentioned in the portion of Beshalach, are designed for this purpose.

The two middle letters of the word *akrav, Kuf* and *Resh*, form the word *kar*, meaning "cold" or "lifeless"—indicating that there is a lifeless aspect to Scorpios. Therefore, the structure of its name, as given by Abraham the patriarch in his book, *Sefer Yetzirah* ("Book of Formation"), was not by chance. The reason the scorpion kills itself is because it does not realize that it has life. Those of us who are not born under the sign of Scorpio understand that we do not want to do anything that could hurt ourselves because we feel our life, we experience our life—and it is dear to us. Therefore, we will do everything in our power to prevent something from disrupting that which is our life.

Scorpios do not have this quality. A Scorpio imagines that they are lifeless, and therefore, like the scorpion, they can sting themselves to death. This is their negative characteristic, and this is where they are not in control. Scorpios are people who, no matter how much suffering they will endure as a result of their actions, are still prepared to go through with it. Does this mean they are selfless people? No, I would rather refer to them as lifeless people because they will not consider themselves when they make decisions that will be injurious to their own health or welfare. Scorpios are not stupid, they are intelligent, emotional, orderly people—so why do they behave in this manner? Like their namesake, a Scorpio does not experience the life-giving force that others in a similar situation will invariably experience. The word *akrav* has not come into this language by accident. As with every other word, it indicates the internal energy-force at its core. The scorpion does not feel the *Or deChochmah* or Light of Wisdom, a term given for the life-giving force inside of us. In the month of Scorpio, this life-giving force cannot be felt unless we are overcoming or rising above the astrological influence of Scorpio to feel the Light—because this life-force is almost non-existent.

Cheshvan is a powerful month. It can create a *mabul*, a devastation. But it does not have to be a bad month—it can also be a month during which we can enjoy the most positivity. The question is one of, are we capable of handling this kind of energy? When Abraham proclaimed Cheshvan to be *mar* or "bitter," he also informed us that, by inverting the letters *mar*, the word becomes *ram*, meaning "exalted." So Cheshvan can also be the most exalted month of the year. The word *mabul* is a code name for the totality of the Tetragrammaton. *Mabul* is made up of the Hebrew letters *Mem, Bet, Vav*, and *Lamed*, which in numerology add up to 78. The number

78 is three times the numerical value of the Tetragrammaton—26 x 3 = 78, indicating the power of a *mabul*.

The onrushing of water is a powerful thing. On the day of Shemini Atzeret, at the end of the month of Tishrei (Libra), we ask that *tal* or "dew" becomes a flow of *geshem* or "rain"—that droplets of dew become a tremendous flow of water into the universe. Without water the universe cannot exist. We are asking for *mabul*, and at the same time we are asking that it be controlled. We do not want to experience a drought but, at the same time, if this water is not controllable, then it is devastating. When the kabbalists suggest people not begin anything during the month of Cheshvan it is because the Bible is merely telling us that in this month there is so much positivity that most people cannot handle it. We would have to be of such a high level of consciousness to be able to handle this tremendous influx of positive energy that has transitioned from droplets of dew into a heavy flow of rain. This is the message.

King Solomon knew that the month of Cheshvan was exalted, and that he could tap into all of this positivity, making it manifest for the entire universe. This is why he wanted the completed vessel of the Temple to be founded in the month of Cheshvan—and herein lies the secret. Both of these two months, Taurus and Scorpio, are a time of excess, an overflow of energy. Rav Shimon decided to leave this world in the month of Iyar because he knew that there was an overabundance of potential energy in this month—and, if not dealt with properly, it could unleash a disaster—as happened with the plague that killed the 24,000 students of Rabbi Akiva.

The Flood began on the 17th day of Cheshvan, which is also a coded message. The number 17 in numerology is *tov* or "good." Now, how do we reconcile "good" with the beginning of the Deluge? It is an apparent contradiction or paradox. Says the Zohar, it is only to teach us that there is no such thing as being lucky or unlucky because, even on a day like *tov*, on the 17th day when it is good, it is not going to be good for everyone. It will be good for some, and bad for some. For Noah, he was saved on that day. For the others, they perished. It is a bad day for those who connect to the negative aspect of that day. Whichever force we are going to tap into depends entirely on us.

We listen to the reading of the Torah on Shabbat Noah because we want to access something that became established in the world—a security shield. When we hear this reading, and connect with God's teachings to Noah about how to protect and create for himself a security shield, we too can get this same instruction for our own lives today.

BOOK OF BERESHEET:

Portion of Lech Lecha

PORTION OF LECH LECHA

Beresheet 12:1 Now the Lord had said to Abram, "Get you out of your country, and from your people, and from your father's household, and go unto the land that I will show you. 2 And I will make you a great nation and I will bless you; I will make your name great, and you will be a blessing. 3 And I will bless those who bless you, and curse whoever curses you; and all families of the earth will be blessed through you."

Abraham (Abram), Chesed, and Destiny

The Bible describes in detail all that Abram did in each verse of the portion of Lech Lecha. It is the story of both Abram and his wife, Sarai, acting with one unified consciousness. Many commentators question the purpose of the phrasing "*lech lecha*," which means "get you out." If Abram was meant simply to leave the land, then the verse could have read "go out." Why say, "get you out."? When we look into the meaning and usage of the Hebrew words, we find there is a deeper meaning in them. But due to an insufficient understanding of the text, the words have long been misinterpreted. If we think we are simply reading a story here, nothing could be further from the truth. This misinterpretation has been with us for 3400 years, and yet what this unique phrasing brings to our attention is that this is *not* a simple story about Abram going out of his land, leaving his birthplace and entering the land that God would reveal to him. If Abram was simply to leave his house, all that would be necessary to express is the one word *lech* or "go out." Moreover, why should Abram go out from his land—what was wrong with it? The Zohar explains that the Sefira of Chesed did not exist at this time, and thus it could not be known. There was no control over the environment. So God was really telling Abram about the consciousness of his land—the main problem being that it did not have any energy that could change consciousness.

Referring to the previous portion of Noah, the Zohar discusses the connection between Malchut and water. The more I delve into the true meaning and nature of water, the more I understand the threat that faces this entire planet. We are literally devouring all the nourishment that the land can provide. I am stating this because if we do not raise our consciousness soon, we will be entirely without food. These days, everything we eat is being genetically modified. The world's supply of fresh water is quickly becoming diminished. A beautiful apple grown without insects may help farmers to grow and sell their produce but what is it they are now selling us? It is not an apple. And it is certainly not a food that the body requires. But then again humankind is capable of restoring the consciousness of Chesed or Mercy.

Let us return to Abram. As we have learned in Kabbalah, Abram is both a patriarch as well as the chariot for drawing down the power of Chesed. The Zohar consistently associates Abraham—as he will be renamed at the end of this section—with the Sefira of Chesed, which is one of the three elements—air (Central Column–Tiferet); water (Right Column–Chesed); and fire (Left Column–Gevurah). Abraham is the conduit of mercy in this world. Without the Zohar we would not have access to this valuable information. Does this then mean that Abraham channels water? After the sin of Adam, and before Abraham, the world had no way in which to rid itself of negativity. It had no way to restore the internal nature of water to what it once was. In other words, the world had no means by which to change its destiny. Thus a flood destroyed the entire planet, as was related in the portion of Noah. After the sin, water lost its connection to its higher nature, and could no longer provide the balance between fire and air. As Abraham himself explains in the *Sefer Yetzirah* ("Book of Formation"), the elements of fire and air were not in balance because it is the energy of water that causes the two to be unified.

The element of water is *chesed* or "sharing." It is because of water that generosity exists in this world. The elements depend on the nature and activity of humankind, and since humanity was corrupt from the very beginning, the entire atmosphere became corrupt, and what followed was the destruction of the entire world. The Mormon Church stresses the necessity of giving and tithing, a concept that has been lost in Judaism, and thus the power to restore consciousness has also been lost. People work hard for their money, and the prevalent way of thinking is: Why should we give it away? One day, the whole world will once again understand the benefit of sharing and tithing, learning that humanity must share and be constantly mindful of the danger of Receiving for Oneself Alone.

The portion of Lecha Lecha, which follows the Tower of Babel incident, serves to teach us how to restore the consciousness of sharing to the world. This section is the first step of drawing *chesed* into this world. Without chesed, without the nature of sharing, the world cannot exist. To change the difficulties the world has endured for 3400 years, we must change. We all fall into certain patterns of reincarnation. Like Abram, our destinies have been formulated to be accompanied by all of their chaos. Yet Abram was told to go out from the land of his forefathers; in effect he is told, "go out from your destiny to the Land of Canaan, the land that I am giving you to inherit." Yet this land is not just another piece of territory. When God told Abram to go from the land of his birthplace, what was He saying? We know that when we are born, our soul is the DNA that describes how we will look, how we will speak, how we will walk—everything about us is included at birth. This is what we come in with. "Get you out," thus teaches us what is spiritually required from us. If we do not alter our DNA, remaining the same as we were at birth, we will then retain all of the baggage from past lives and its effects. Our DNA has been designed for us with some of the good things in life but also with those terrible aspects of chaos. We need to flip the switch in our mind and transform our fundamental nature, thereby removing the baggage.

Our judgments govern our influence over the environment. Look at your life and ask yourself if you have ever deviated from what society decided for you. This includes what your children and relatives have determined to be the way you must behave. Until we begin to change from being comfortable, and start to assume a consciousness where we are in control of our choices, everything in our lives will remain the same. This is why nothing has changed for humanity in 3400 years, and the same chaos reappears from generation to generation. The date and location maybe different, but we all fall back into the same patterns. Very few of us ask if we can change the world. The goal is not to change the whole world but rather that each of us takes responsibility for our own actions in it. In this sense, the removal of chaos *is* our responsibility. People say, "With all the problems I have in my life, how can I remove chaos from the world?" But no one says you must remove it. What the Bible is suggesting is that if we think we have had enough of chaos, then "get you out" is the procedure to remove it. This is the consciousness that is required. Then, and only then, as each individual changes, can the world experience change.

When God said to Abram, "I will bless those who bless you, and I will curse those who curse you," this was because Abram was exceptional; he could influence and inspire the entire world by his actions. There was no other reason for God to say, "I will bless and I will curse." People think this is the nature of God—One Who blesses and One Who curses. This corruption has remained for 3400 years. We do not ask ourselves if we are discussing a God Who has a quality of mercy, do we? Instead people say, "God in his mysterious way knows what He is doing." Thereby we foolishly remain in chaos thinking that this is our lot. The Bible never *demands*; the Bible and Kabbalah only *suggest*. If you want to change a life of chaos into one of beneficence then there are instruments—tools by which we can change our destiny. When the Bible says that the whole world will be blessed because of Abraham, it is to indicate that, to the extent we can draw down the positivity of Sefira Chesed—as Abraham did—each of us can make a difference. We can reach out into that power. The force of Chesed transcends masses of people and consequently, says scripture, not only Abraham will be blessed but the whole world as well. The whole world exists in chaos because of those who refuse to *choose* to remove chaos. We all want to be blessed, yet when we are thinking only of our own blessings and not of the world's blessings, it does not work. God has created a flawless system, and we need to understand it so that it can function for us.

Seeing Things as They Are

We are essentially in a prison of our five senses. Born in this prison, our senses become instruments that keep us from understanding what is actually around us. What the eye sees is so little of what is really there. To see this world as it truly is we need to remove these barriers. When we see something beautiful, we so often project other qualities onto it—such as goodness or value. Is this assumption necessarily true? No, of course not. You cannot judge a book by its cover. Most of the time, the outward appearance of things is somewhat deceptive. This section is here to give us the ability to reach higher levels of consciousness, to see things as they actually are. Time, space, and motion are a handicap to which we are very devoted in this Earthly sphere. Yet we have an innate ability to travel without the restraints of three-dimensional reality. We need to break through these constraints.

Is a person born with an evil inclination? Are we all essentially evil—even as little children? Is this what the scripture is trying to tell us? No, what we can learn from it is that we are all in a prison whose bars are time, space, and motion. Imagine if we could see what is really around us. Few people would commit negative acts if everyone could see beyond the area of limitation and thus knew their intentions beforehand. In this portion, we are not particularly interested in knowing that Abram moved from one place to another but rather we are interested in the knowledge that this reading gives us to achieve mastery over our own destiny.

4 So Abram departed, as the Lord had spoken to him; and Lot went with him. And Abram was seventy-five years old when he departed from Haran. 5 And Abram took his wife Sarai, and Lot, his brother's son, and all their possessions that they had accumulated, and the souls they had acquired in Haran, and they set out for the land of Canaan, and into the Land of Canaan they came. 6 And Abram passed through the land to the place of Sichem in the plain of Moreh. And the Canaanites were in the land. 7 And the Lord appeared to Abram and said, "To your seed I will give this land." And there he built an altar to the Lord, who had appeared to him. 8 And from there he went to the mountain east of Bethel and pitched his tent, having Bethel on the west and Hai on the east. And there he built an altar to the Lord and called on the name of the Lord.

The Evil Eye

This portion touches on the primacy of the individual, and what we have been given to alleviate the chaos in our lives. Everyone in the world has a lack. If we had come into this world perfect, then why come here to live a given number of years and then leave? It does not stand to reason that this could be the purpose of life. We all come into this world lacking something. Adam and Eve were forbidden to eat from the Tree of Knowledge, just as we are deprived of what we desire in our own lives. What was the purpose of the deprivation of Adam and Eve? Immortality. Was life as sweet after they ate from the Tree of Knowledge? No. This is the case with the evil eye. We do not intend to create a situation where someone possessing something has to lose it because of our own lack—and yet we do it all the same. Even in the closest communities we have to contend with the evil eye. Even Abram had to contend with all the wars. And yet what took place 4000 years ago demonstrates the power of the individual, and encourages us to achieve our full potential, even though the odds are stacked against us.

The Bible gives us absolutes, not probabilities. In this physical world everything has a "margin of error." There is a probability of success, but with no guarantees. Our lives are lived this way because we came into this world lacking. The evil eye, which can be a result of this lack, is always a lose-lose situation—in fact it is the only situation that is always lose-lose. At least in the case of physical robbery, the victim loses something and the thief gains it, if only temporarily. Unfortunately, this is not the case when we rob someone of energy. We are not aware that there is spiritual robbery taking place, when we see that someone has something we lack—thus activating the evil eye. It is human nature to often feel that we are missing out on something in life—that we do not have all we want, and so we wish for that which another person has. However, this way of thinking is the surest way of never getting the very thing we want.

When a person, experiencing a lack, thinks if only they could have what he or she has, this thought sucks a little energy from the person who has what they want. The person with the lack does not get anything or benefit at all from this evil eye, and moreover they can come to doubt whether they will ever acquire what they desire. When we want what someone else has, we are in a sense stealing the energy of having, yet we do not receive anything for this.

Abraham did not possess an evil eye, and he underwent ten tests including being thrown into a fiery pit, where the fire could not consume him. This is because Abraham was totally uninvolved with himself, for he embodied Chesed, and Chesed is the essence of water and the force of sharing. How can we give that which we do not have? In working on changing our consciousness, we work to attain this level of transformation, we work to truly share. We can only share that which we have, and if we are at the level of feeling lack, true sharing is difficult to achieve. If we do not have peace and certainty within, if we do not feel complete, how can we share? The true test is to assess where we are is to check in with how we feel when we witness someone else experiencing success or joy. Are we truly happy for them with no ulterior motive? Do we think how we can help them to have even more fulfillment in their lives? Or do we become self-involved, comparing what we do not have with their surfeit?

The consciousness of sharing is what Abraham embodied. This is why he is Chesed. We need to start seeing our cup as half-full and not the opposite, half-empty. Appreciation is how we can get there at every moment. In the Study of the Four Phases, Rav Ashlag said that until you can be happy for your neighbor in their blessings with no agenda you will remain in a lose-lose situation. It is important to cultivate the understanding that our own good lies in having the consciousness of feeling pleasure at the good fortune of another. This is the way we can obtain what we are missing. But our circumstances may not change immediately. Someone said to me recently, "I've been at the Centre eight years and I still haven't found my soulmate." My question for them was: "What did you receive after eight years of being at the Centre?" The issue is one of knowing precisely what we are gaining from whatever activity we pursue. Fulfillment in life works on one principle—certainty.

9 Then Abram journeyed and continued toward the south. 10 And there was a famine in the land, and Abram went down to Egypt to live there because the famine was dire in the land. 11 And it came to pass, as he was about to enter Egypt, he said to his wife Sarai, "Behold now, I know what a fair woman you are. 12 Therefore it will come to pass that when the Egyptians see you, they will say, 'This is his wife.' And they will kill me but will let you live. 13 Say, I pray you, that you are my sister, so that I will be treated well for your sake and my soul will be spared because of you." 14 And it came to pass that when Abram came to Egypt, the Egyptians saw that she was a very fair woman. 15 And the princes of Pharaoh saw her, and they praised her to Pharaoh, and the woman was taken into Pharaoh's house. 16 And he treated Abram well for her sake, and he acquired sheep and oxen, and asses, and menservants and maidservants, and she-asses, and camels. 17 And the Lord inflicted plagues on Pharaoh and his house because of Sarai, Abram's wife. 18 And Pharaoh called for Abram and said, "What is this that you have done to me? Why didn't you tell me she was your wife? 19 Why did you say, 'She is my sister,' so that I may have taken her to be my wife? Now, therefore, here is your wife. Take her and go on your way." 20 And Pharaoh commanded his men concerning Abram, and they sent him away, and his wife, and everything that he had.

Beresheet 13:1 And Abram went up out of Egypt, with his wife and everything that he had, and Lot went with him into the south. 2 And Abram was very wealthy in cattle, in silver, and in gold. 3 And he went on his journeys from the south until he came to Bethel, to the place where his tent had been at the beginning, between Bethel and Hai; 4 and to the place where he had first built the altar. And there Abram called on the name of the Lord. 5 And Lot, who went with Abram, also had flocks, and herds, and tents. 6 And the land was not able to bear them that they might dwell together, for their substance was great, so that they could not dwell together. 7 And there was strife between Abram's herdsmen and the herdsmen of Lot. And the Canaanites and Perizzites also dwelled in the land. 8 And Abram said to Lot, "Let there be no strife between you and me, I pray you, or between my herdsmen and your herdsmen, for we are brethren. 9 Is not the whole land before you? Separate yourself from me, I pray you. If you will take the left hand, then I will go to the right; or if you depart to the right hand, then I will go to the left." 10 And Lot lifted up his eyes and saw the whole plain of Jordan and that it was well watered, before the Lord destroyed Sodom and Gomorrah, even like the garden of the Lord, like the land of Egypt, as you come to Zo'ar. 11 So Lot chose for himself the whole plain of Jordan and Lot journeyed east. And they separated themselves, the one from the other. 12 Abram lived in the land of Canaan, while Lot lived in the cities of the plain and pitched his tent towards Sodom. 13 But the men of Sodom were wicked and were sinning greatly against the Lord. 14 And the Lord said to Abram after Lot had separated from him, "Lift up your eyes from where you are and look north and south, east and west. 15 All the land that you see I will give to you and to your seed forever. 16 And I will make your seed like the dust of the earth, so that if a man could count the dust, then your seed could be counted. 17 Arise, walk through the length and breadth of the land, for I will give it to you." 18 Then Abram removed his tent and went and dwelt in the plain of Mamre, which is in Hebron, and he built there an altar to the Lord.

Beresheet 14:1 And it came to pass in the days of Amraphel, king of Shinar, Arioch, king of Ellasar, Chedorlo'amer, king of Elam, and Tidal, king of nations; 2 that they went to war against Bera, king of Sodom, and with Birsha, king of Gomorrah, Shinab, king of Admah, Shemeber, king of Zeboi'im, and the king of Bela, which is Zo'ar. 3 All these latter kings joined forces in the Valley of Siddim, which is the Salt Sea. 4 Twelve years they served Chedorla'omer, and in the thirteenth year they rebelled. 5 And in the fourteenth year, Chedorla'omer and the kings allied with him smote the Rephaites in Ashteroth-Karna'im, the Zuzites in Ham,

the Emites in Shaveh Kiri'atha'im, 6 and
the Horites in their mount Seir, to Elparan
which is by the wilderness. 7 And they
returned and came to Enmishpat, which is
Kadesh, and they smote the whole country
of the Amalekites, and also the Amorites
who were living in Hazazontamar. 8 And the
king of Sodom, and the king of Gomorrah,
and the king of Admah, and the king of
Zeboi'im and the king of Bela (Zo'ar) joined
each other to battle with them in the Valley
of Siddim; 9 against Chedorla'omer, king of
Elam, and with Tidal, king of nations, and
Amraphel, king of Shinar, and Arioch, king
of Ellasar—four kings against five. 10 And
the Valley of Siddim was full of slime pits,
and the kings of Sodom and Gomorrah fled
and fell there, and those that survived fled to
the mountain. 11 And they (the four kings)
took all the goods of Sodom and Gomorrah
and all their victuals, and went on their way.
12 They also took Lot, Abram's brother's
son who dwelt in Sodom, and his goods and
departed. 13 And one who had escaped came
and told Abram, the Hebrew; for he dwelt in
the plain of Mamre the Amorite, brother of
Eshcol and brother of Aner; and they were
allied with Abram. 14 And when Abram
heard that his brethren was taken captive,
he armed his trained servants, born in his
own house, 318 of them, and pursued them
to Dan. 15 And he divided himself and his
servants from them during the night, and
smote them, and he chased them to Hobah,

which is on the left hand of Damascus. 16 He brought back all the goods and also brought back his brethren Lot and his goods, together with the women and the people. 17 And the king of Sodom went out to meet him when he returned from defeating Chedorla'omer and the kings that were with him, at the Valley of Shaveh, which is the King's Valley.

The Problem of War

This scripture says that four kings and their nations conducted war with five kings and their respective nations. It is significant that it does not state the reason for the war, but simply indicates that war occurred. With the story of war and chaos in this section, we are to understand that both sides had reasons—we can all find a justification for what we want to do, whether it is something that can hurt or help others. In the case of war it has become accepted that the enemy deserves to be annihilated. The question of who is "right" and who is "wrong" does not enter into it. Moreover, even with all the justifications for war, fear of war remains, especially as we witness its aftermath—parents lose children, children lose parents, loved ones are left behind to live without the ones they loved. History has taught us that force for *any* well-intentioned reasons, like the removal of a dictatorship, will not end the need for more war. Without question, whether one side is right and the other is wrong, war is evil. Evil in the Name of God, evil in the name of freedom are both evil because ultimately both will result in innocent victims on either side of the battle. Let us not lose sight of the obvious conclusion that even if we can remove a few dictators or terrorists, the world's problems are not going to be ended. There will still be violence and crime. These problems did not arrive today. The reason I stress this is because we are all waiting for the day that evildoers are captured and removed from existence. Remember, the chaos that was created will persist, since it does not end with the removal of any physical body.

Kabbalistically, we want to think not only about the entire picture but also about what lies ahead. Will we eradicate chaos with war? Will our situation be improved? Will we come to a time of happiness and freedom from chaos? No. This scripture is pointing out that war is evil. Freedom is the key. But what is freedom and how is it achieved? How long does such peace last—50 years, 100 years at most? Is that all civilization is about? We need to do away with war as the methodology by which humanity can achieve freedom from chaos, pain, and suffering. The removal of the perpetrator will not remove the pain of those who have already suffered. With the story of war and chaos in this section, scripture wants to tell us that both sides had reasons and that unfortunately, we are more prone to see only from our own perspective. We must go beyond the one percent, as well as the common ideas about reality, and try to fathom what we could accomplish if we could raise the level of our consciousness above our limitations.

For so long now, humankind has accepted the idea that we must suffer, and so we try to bear the suffering. The Lightforce must be brought to bear for all of humankind—only then will chaos end.

Abram's Rescue of Lot

Abram heard that his nephew, Lot, had been captured in the war between the nine nations—a war that went on for years. What did Abram do? Though he heard that Sodom had thousands of soldiers, he gathered his entire household of 318 people to do battle against the soldiers of Sodom, and he defeated them. Why do we treat this as merely a simple story? What is important, and why pay attention to the number 318? The kabbalists explain that the number 318 is the numerical value of the name "Eliezer," which means "God is help," indicating that Abram invoked the help of God for this battle.

18 And Melchizedek, king of Salem, brought out bread and wine. He was the priest of the most high God, 19 and he blessed him, saying, "Blessed be Abram of the most high God, Creator of heaven and earth. 20 And blessed be the most high God, who delivered your enemies into your hand." And he gave him tithes of everything. 21 And the king of Sodom said to Abram, "Give me the people and keep the goods for yourself." 22 And Abram said to the king of Sodom, "I have lifted up my hand to the Lord, the most high God, Creator of Heaven and Earth, 23 that I will take nothing from a thread to a shoe-latchet, and that I will not take anything belonging to you, lest you should say, 'I made Abram rich.' 24 Only that which the young men have eaten, and the portion of the men that went with me, Aner, Eshcol, and Mamre, let them take their share.

Beresheet 15:1 After these things, the word of the Lord came to Abram in a vision saying, "Fear not, Abram. I am your shield, and your exceedingly great reward." 2 And Abram said, "Lord God, what can You give me, since I remain childless and the steward of my house is Eliezer of Damascus?" 3 And Abram said, "Behold to me You have given no seed; and so a servant born in my house is my heir." 4 And behold, the word of the Lord came to him saying, "This man will not be your heir, but he that will come from your own body will be your heir." 5 And He took

him outside and said, "Look now toward heaven and tell the stars, if you can count them." And He said to him, "So shall your seed be." 6 And he believed the Lord, and he counted it to him as righteousness.

Control over the Stars and Planets

We have, in this section, the assurance from God that we can exert control over the influence of the stars. God told Abraham to go outside, look up into the sky and count the stars—so numerous would be his children. What God was saying is that we can control the influence of the planets and the stars. Humanity has not yet recognized that we as individuals can control our destiny. We have believed that this power is in the hands of the authorities—whoever they may be. The portion of Lech Lecha teaches us that we have been given the ability and the tools to control the influence of the stars and planets, if we are open to it.

7 And He also said to him, "I am the Lord, who brought you out of Ur of the Chaldeans to give you this land to inherit it." 8 And he said, "Lord God, whereby will I inherit it?" 9 And He said to him, "Bring Me a heifer of three years old, and a she-goat of three years old, and a ram of three years old, and a dove and a young pigeon." 10 And he brought all these to Him, and he divided them in two and arranged the halves opposite each other; but the birds he did not divide. 11 And when the fowls came down on the carcasses, Abram drove them away. 12 And when the sun was going down, a deep sleep fell upon Abram, and a dreadful darkness came over him. 13 And He said to Abram, "Know for certain that your seed will be strangers in a land that is not their own, and they will serve them and they will be mistreated four hundred years. 14 And also that nation that they will serve, will I judge, and afterward they will come out with great substance. 15 And you will go to your fathers in peace and you will be buried at a good old age. 16 But in the fourth generation your descendants will come back here, for the iniquity of the Amorites is not yet full." 17 And it came to pass that when the sun went down, and it was dark, a smoking furnace and a burning lamp appeared and passed between the pieces. 18 On that same day the Lord made a covenant with Abram and said, "To your seed I give this land, from the river of Egypt to the great river, the Euphrates: 19 the Kenites,

and the Kenizzites, and the Kadmonites,
20 and the Hittites, and the Perizzites, and
the Rephaites, 21 and the Amorites, and the
Canaanites, and the Girgashites and the
Jebusites."

Beresheet 16:1 Now Sarai, Abram's wife,
had borne him no children. But she had an
Egyptian maidservant named Hagar; 2 And
Sarai said to Abram, "The Lord has kept
me from having children. Go, sleep with my
maidservant; perhaps I can build a family
through her." Abram agreed to what Sarai
said. 3 So after Abram had been living in
Canaan ten years, Sarai his wife took her
Egyptian maidservant Hagar and gave her to
her husband to be his wife. 4 He slept with
Hagar, and she conceived. When she knew
she was pregnant, she began to despise her
mistress. 5 Then Sarai said to Abram, "You
are responsible for the wrong I am suffering.
I put my servant in your arms, and now that
she knows she is pregnant, she despises me.
May the Lord judge between you and me." 6
"Your servant is in your hands," Abram said.
"Do with her whatever you think best." Then
Sarai mistreated Hagar; so she fled from her.
7 The angel of the Lord found Hagar near a
spring in the desert; it was the spring that
is beside the road to Shur. 8 And he said,
"Hagar, servant of Sarai, where have you
come from, and where are you going?" "I'm
running away from my mistress, Sarai,"
she answered. 9 Then the angel of the Lord

told her, "Go back to your mistress and submit to her." 10 The angel added, "I will so increase your descendants that they will be too numerous to count." 11 The angel of the Lord also said to her: "You are now with child and you will have a son. You shall name him Ishmael, for the Lord has heard of your misery. 12 He will be a wild donkey of a man; his hand will be against everyone and everyone's hand against him, and he will live in hostility toward all his brothers." 13 She gave this name to the Lord who spoke to her: "You are the God who sees me," for she said, "I have now seen the One who sees me." 14 This is why the well was called Beer Lahai Roi; it is still there, between Kadesh and Bered. 15 So Hagar bore Abram a son, and Abram gave the name Ishmael to the son she had borne. 16 Abram was eighty-six years old when Hagar bore him Ishmael.

Evil Eye, Hagar, and Ishmael

Abraham was eighty six when Hagar gave birth to the original Arabic nation of Islam in the person of Ishmael. This portion contains the story of Abraham impregnating the handmaiden Hagar, and tells us that Sarai, as she was first named, forced her to leave. Though she had insisted on the coupling herself, Sarai was not happy after her maidservant became pregnant. She told Abram that Hagar looked upon her in a demeaning way. "May God judge between you and me," (Beresheet 16:5) refers to her handmaiden. There is a dot in the text above the word "judge," and, in the Hebrew language, dots are only generally found where there is a vowel. This unique placement of the dot is there to teach us something. In the story, Abram told Sarai to do whatever she believed to be right, and she sent Hagar away into the wilderness, where she could have died. However, an angel came to assist Hagar and Ishmael. The commentators say that the reason for the dot is because of *ayin hara* or "evil eye." We know that the eye can generate evil and create a deficiency for the ones of whom we are jealous. Even a compliment can be a carrier of the evil eye, concealing, as it can do, a dissatisfaction with one's own lack when compared with the abundance of another. It is the thought or intention behind a compliment that determines whether or not it carries evil eye.

Beresheet 17:1 When Abram was ninety-nine years old, the Lord appeared to Abram and said to him, "I am God Almighty; walk before Me and be you perfect. 2 And I will make My covenant between Me and you and will multiply you exceedingly." 3 And Abram fell on his face, and God talked with him saying, 4 "As for Me, this is My covenant with you: You will be a father of many nations. 5 No longer will you be called Abram; your name will be Abraham, for I have made you a father of many nations. 6 I will make you exceedingly fruitful; and I will make nations of you, and kings will come out of you. 7 And I will establish My covenant between Me and you and your seed after you for the generations to come, as an everlasting covenant to be your God to you and to your seed after you. 8 And I will give to you and to your seed after you the land in which you are a stranger, all the land of Canaan, for an everlasting possession; and I will be their God." 9 And God said to Abraham, "You must keep My covenant, you and your seed after you for the generations to come. 10 This is My covenant you shall keep, between Me and you and your seed after you: Every male child among you shall be circumcised. 11 And you will circumcise the flesh of your foreskin and it will be the sign of the covenant between Me and you. 12 And he that is eight days old shall be circumcised among you, every man child in your generations, he that is born in the

house, or bought with money of any stranger that is not of thy seed.

The Importance of the Eighth Day

Why is it necessary to perform a circumcision (*brit milah*) on the eighth day? The Zohar, in the portion of Tazria, explains that Beresheet One contains the precedents for the manner in which things operate in our universe. As it is written in the Study of the Ten Luminous Emanations by Rav Ashlag, before anything can become actualized it goes through a process of seven stages—meaning that the Seven Days of Creation are the first Seven Sefirot. In Beresheet Two, when Adam was created on a physical level—when he became actualized—seven vessels had become established. Following this, the soul becomes "imprisoned" within a body. Imprisoned because of the dichotomy between soul and body. The soul is of a Desire to Receive for the Sake of Sharing. The body has an opposite characteristic, a Desire to Receive for the Self Alone. How do these two opposites become united as one operating actualization of the soul? The Zohar explains that the soul becomes actualized following the establishment of the Seven Sefirot—the seven aspects of a complete Vessel. Seven particular aspects of energies are established within the physical frame we call the newborn, then the soul is united and becomes part of the body. The soul must first find its habitat on the metaphysical level before it can become actualized. This unification between the soul and the body cannot, and does not, take place until the eighth day because until that day a soul does not have the proper vessel by which it can become enclothed in flesh.

The body is nothing without a soul. Death means the soul has left. The body has no function by and of itself beyond the energy it receives when the soul makes its presence felt. There must be a completion of seven days before this force called the soul can become manifest. The moment the soul becomes manifest within a body, the Lightforce becomes manifest and the foreskin that was created takes on the embodiment of negativity. The Zohar says that to permit an unobstructed flowing of energy necessitates involving the Satan. In other words, each individual male must have its counterpart. If there is a soul, the antithesis of that soul must also be present. One without the other cannot exist. Satan's ultimate desire is to draw to itself any energy, since this is the lifeblood of negative energy. It can only take energy from something that is positive, like the soul. If the soul is not there, it has no purpose. So if the foreskin is removed, on the fifth or sixth day, we are, in effect, removing a foreskin that is without internal energy. If the soul is not there and Satan has nothing to feed from, then Satan consciousness is not there either. Only on the eighth day, when the soul ultimately finds its place and is united with the body, does Satan's negative energy also settle into its place, which is called the foreskin. The Satan is manifest in the foreskin on the eighth day, not before. If the foreskin is removed before the eighth day, all that has taken place is a piece of skin has simply been removed, but the effect of removing Satan has not occurred.

The *brit milah* should be performed as early as possible in the morning of the eighth day. It is not performed in the afternoon or at a time that is convenient. This is a serious operation, therefore we do it in the morning, when the energy-intelligence of Chesed or Mercy prevails in the universe. This means we perform this important spiritual surgery on our own turf and not on Satan's turf. The afternoon is the negative part of the day, and in that it has affinity with Satan and is thus his part of the day. We also do not perform a circumcision at night because this is when demons have dominion. Of course, in this instance we are discussing a healthy infant. There are, however, many times when baby boys are born a little yellow—they are jaundiced. One should depend on a very competent *mohel* because he knows more than the medical professional with regard to whether or not a child is capable of withstanding the *brit milah*. The one who should be consulted first and foremost is the *mohel*, and if he says the decision should be left to the doctor, then it should be left to the doctor. Circumcision can therefore sometimes be delayed both by the *mohel* and the doctor, who agree that the child is not able to have the procedure at this time. This delay represents a problem because Satan is now present and, as a result, he is now being given an opportunity to entrench himself. The Zohar explains that this is not a question of whether it is fair or not for the child because the reason for a child whose circumcision is delayed is based on his prior incarnation. There is a *tikkun* (spiritual correction) process for this particular child and, therefore, he is placed in a certain environment with its set of circumstances whereby he can ultimately achieve his *tikkun*. Part of his *tikkun* is to be faced with the problem that the Satan has been given an opportunity to become entrenched because he was not removed right at the onset. Therefore, when problems occur, and they will occur, this will only be an opportunity for the child to overcome them. If he has studied reincarnation and the true significance of circumcision, he will be better equipped to deal with whatever is happening, and know why the situation is happening, and can seek the methods by which he can extricate himself from his problems.

In his Introduction to the Zohar, Rav Ashlag discusses 14 of the 613 Precepts he considers to be the most important, meaning, those that affect the cosmos to a greater degree than others. One of those 14 Precepts is to circumcise on the eighth day—to remove the defilement of the foreskin. To have Malchut, which is the ultimate Vessel, without defilement we need to go through all of the procedures of the *brit milah*. I think it is vital that we discuss the process of circumcision in depth because many people today do not know the proper meditation that should be applied going into this procedure. It is so important that the *mohel* knows what he is doing spiritually as much as he is does physically, in surgically removing the foreskin.

13 He that is born in your house, and he that is bought with your money, must be circumcised: and My covenant shall be in your flesh for an everlasting covenant. 14 And the uncircumcised male child, whose flesh of his foreskin is not circumcised, that soul will be cut off from his people; he has broken My covenant."

The Brit Milah

Here we have mention of the most significant tool with which to eliminate the chaos in this world. As we have learned in Kabbalah, the *brit milah* or circumcision removes the strongest concentration of negative consciousness that is assembled anywhere in this universe—the foreskin—giving us an opportunity to remove it and bury it. With this portion, we are faced with an opportunity that I hope will be recognized.

15 And God said to Abraham, "As for Sarai, your wife, you are no longer to call her Sarai; her name will be Sarah. 16 And I will bless her and will give you a son by her. I will bless her and she will be a mother of nations; kings of peoples will come from her." 17 Then Abraham fell on his face; and laughed and said in his heart, "Will a child be born to a man that is a hundred years old? And will Sarah bear a child at the age of ninety?" 18 And Abraham said to God, "If only Ishmael might live before You!" 19 Then God said, "Yes, but your wife Sarah will bear you a son, and you will call him Isaac. And I will establish My covenant with him as an everlasting covenant and with his seed after him. 20 And as for Ishmael, I have heard you: Behold I have blessed him; and I will make him fruitful and will multiply him exceedingly. Twelve princes will he give birth to and I will make him into a great nation. 21 But My covenant I will establish with Isaac, whom Sarah will bear to you by this time next year." 22 And He left off talking with him, and God went up from Abraham.

The Miracle of Regeneration

Here we have another aspect of the Abram and Sarai story. At this point, Sarai was a woman 90 years of age, and Abram was 100 years old, and God told them of a miracle that was about to take place. Abram and Sarai were told to undergo a name change, and the Hebrew letter *Hei* was inserted into both their names, making them now Abraham and Sarah. Because of this name change their destiny would be changed. Sarai was not only 90 years old, she had no reproductive organs. Even that physical handicap can be altered. Women today are giving birth later and later in life. This change of destiny is another case of mind over matter. The mind can produce organs, the mind can restructure matter. From the Zohar we learn that, as we get closer to the end of time as we know it, the "movie" called chaos will come to an end. This movie will no longer be a big hit. Missing reproductive organs will re-form, and severed limbs will grow back. How do we know this will be a reality? People who have lost limbs still feel them—a phenomenon where something that is not there feels like it is there.

The kabbalists knew 4000 years ago that when the heart or liver first grew it was DNA that created these organs. Our skin, hair and nails grow back, so why not other parts of the body? We are limiting our consciousness to what it believes to be true. But appearances are deceptive. Our consciousness has not achieved its full potential, so in effect we are still in prison. The scripture here is telling us that a change of name can change the physical reality of a person, so should we all change our names? I would have to write a whole new chapter on the concept of destiny to answer this question. Our name represents the 99 Percent Reality of who we are. When a soul name is lacking, as we believe is the case with an individual experiencing an undue amount of pain, then we can consider using this tool. The 99 percent of the soul, which is consciousness, is profoundly affected by the name that is given.

23 And Abraham took Ishmael, his son, and all those born in his house and all that were bought with his money, every male among the men of Abraham's house, and circumcised the flesh of their foreskin on that same day, as God had said to him. 24 And Abraham was ninety-nine years old when he was circumcised in the flesh of his foreskin. 25 And his son Ishmael was thirteen years old when he was circumcised in the flesh of his foreskin. 26 On that same day, Abraham and his son Ishmael were both circumcised. 27 And all the men of his house, born in the house and bought with money of the stranger, were circumcised with him.

The Power of Circumcision: Brit Milah

We return to the topic of circumcision, which, unfortunately, is considered irrelevant, and is thus being ignored. What is circumcision? It demonstrates the covenant between man and God. If someone does not do a *brit milah*, is he not connected to God? The *brit milah* serves to release that God-given natural ability to be part of God, to act like God. The kabbalist says we were born a part of God. When Adam was created, he was made in the likeness of God, and we are as well. We all know that God can do anything. God can create miracles, and we, too, can create miracles, yet if miracles do not happen for us, it is not God's fault.

The truth of the matter is that we have not demonstrated our likeness to God. Is God a purveyor of evil? No, the kabbalists told us 4000 years ago that God has but one nature and that is of sharing. Therefore, if we are experiencing chaos, we know that we are shutting ourselves off from the Lightforce of God. We are like a person in a room who does not know that a light is out and stumbles over all the furniture. What we intend to do with this reading is to bring the Lightforce of God into our lives, so we can finally see ourselves for who we are—part of God.

When God told us in this text to perform circumcision, He made a pact with humanity to be part of the structure of human existence. The existence of evil was and is present, and that force of evil is what turns many of us toward negative activity directed at our fellow beings. The kabbalists say that through the foreskin is encapsulated the highest degree of negativity. By commanding us to perform circumcision, God has thereby given us an opportunity to remove negativity for the benefit of humankind. This is a powerful methodology that enables us to remove a large portion of the negativity surrounding us. Today, all too often, circumcision is not performed in a spiritually correct manner, and because of this we have lost the greatest opportunity to remove pain and suffering from our lives and the world. Kabbalah is not a religion but rather a technology to manage the negativity in this world so it does not control humanity.

This is the case with Abraham: The world around him was corrupt, and life was lived then much as it is today. Kabbalah reminds us continually of Abraham, who is the power of unity. Unfortunately, in this world the power of unity is accompanied by the aspect of negativity. This is the way the world was established. In the most powerful organ of the human body, the organ that can produce a new life, therein also lies the accumulation of all that Satan can bring upon us in the way of chaos.

Today, there is a tendency to be against circumcision both for non-Jews and Jews alike—and so a most powerful tool is being lost.

Abraham: The Epitome of Sharing

Even though Abram was Chesed he also had as his companion the *orla* or "foreskin," which is the embodiment of Satan. In this world, it requires a constant effort to remove Satan from our lives. But we are given tools and opportunities to keep this force of negativity under control. The *brit milah*, when performed correctly, is the most powerful one of all. However, having a properly performed *brit milah* does not put us on easy street. Life is still a struggle. As long as we do not permanently bury that Satan aspect in us, as long as there remains even the tiniest measure within, we have him as our constant companion. And so, Abraham performed this miracle of circumcision, and because of this action the world received another tool to remove chaos.

The Importance of Circumcision

Where is the first mention of circumcision in the Bible? In Beresheet 16, in the portion of Lech Lecha, we find Sarai suggesting to Abram that he take their maidservant for a wife since they were childless, so that Hagar would be able to bear a child for Abram. The Bible tells us in Beresheet 16:16: "And Abram was 86 years old when Hagar gave birth to Ishmael." Of what significance is it to us how old Abram was when he fathered a child? Then in Beresheet 17, 13 years later, when Abram was 99 years old, there is a change of Abram's name. Beresheet 17:5 says, "Neither shall thy name anymore be called Abram, but thy name shall be Abraham"—there was the addition of the Hebrew letter *Hei* inserted into his name. In verses 11-12, it says, "And you shall be circumcised in the flesh of your foreskin, and it shall be a covenant between Me and you. And be it that a child that is eight days old shall be circumcised amongst you." Here we have the beginning of one of the 613 Precepts concerning circumcision. Why does circumcision have to be considered the *brit* or "covenant" between the Lord and Abraham, and subsequently all of Israel? The Bible also mentions that Abraham was 99, and Ishmael was 13, when he circumcised himself and Ishmael. Consequently, to this very day, all descendants of Ishmael, namely the Arabs, circumcise their sons at age 13.

Another point I would like to mention, before we delve further into the importance of circumcision, is that when in Beresheet 17:23 it says, "And Abraham circumcised the entire household, the flesh of their foreskin in that day," which day was it? Here we have another indication that the circumcision must take place "on that day," meaning not before the eighth day. We also know that if circumcision takes place before the eighth day, it is completely invalid and another aspect of the *brit milah* must then again be performed after the foreskin has been removed. This is known as "the drawing of a little blood," which is done by a *mohel*, the one who is knowledgeable in the performance of circumcision. When we discuss a precept, we know that its purpose is not a biblical doctrine. It is not merely for the sake of God thrusting another instruction upon us—as if we have not got enough of them already.

The Zohar says there is a reason the Creator put Abraham through this sequence of events, with his name change and circumcision. Why did Abraham have the circumcision and change his name at 99 years old, rather than at 86? What is the significance of 86? *Elokim*, one of the Names of God that is connected more closely with this physical world—which which contains both good and evil—has the numerical value of 86. The Tetragrammaton—*Yud, Hei, Vav, Hei*—is a pure energy force connected to the Tree of Life that always has an intrinsic characteristic of a positive force—there is no evil side to the force of the Tetragrammaton. There is however, an evil side to *Elokim*. The Zohar says that, although Abraham represents Chesed, there is also an extension of Abraham that, while it is Chesed, came about because he was 86 years old and had not yet achieved the Chesed consciousness that would come at the age of 99. At age 86, Abram was still not involved in a pure Chesed consciousness. There was, therefore, a rebirth for Abraham with his new name. There was a completely new Abraham, one of a pure Chesed consciousness. At that point, when he was overcome with this transformation, he was ready for a new kind of quality, which was Chesed—thus the circumcision was required at this time and not before.

About the Centres

Kabbalah is the deepest and most hidden meaning of the Torah or Bible. Through the ultimate knowledge and mystical practices of Kabbalah, one can reach the highest spiritual levels attainable. Although many people rely on belief, faith, and dogmas in pursuing the meaning of life, Kabbalists seek a spiritual connection with the Creator and the forces of the Creator, so that the strange becomes familiar, and faith becomes knowledge.

Throughout history, those who knew and practiced the Kabbalah were extremely careful in their dissemination of the knowledge because they knew the masses of mankind had not yet prepared for the ultimate truth of existence. Today, kabbalists know that it is not only proper but necessary to make the Kabbalah available to all who seek it.

The Research Centre of Kabbalah is an independent, non-profit institute founded in Israel in 1922. The Centre provides research, information, and assistance to those who seek the insights of Kabbalah. The Centre offers public lectures, classes, seminars, and excursions to mystical sites at branches in Israel and in the United States. Branches have been opened in Mexico, Montreal, Toronto, Paris, Hong Kong, and Taiwan.

Our courses and materials deal with the Zoharic understanding of each weekly portion of the Torah. Every facet of life is covered and other dimensions, hithertofore unknown, provide a deeper connection to a superior reality. Three important beginner courses cover such aspects as: Time, Space and Motion; Reincarnation, Marriage, Divorce; Kabbalistic Meditation; Limitation of the Five Senses; Illusion-Reality; Four Phases; Male and Female, Death, Sleep, Dreams; Food; and Shabbat.

Thousands of people have benefited from the Centre's activities, and the Centre's publishing of kabbalistic material continues to be the most comprehensive of its kind in the world, including translations in English, Hebrew, Russian, German, Portuguese, French, Spanish, Farsi (Persian).

Kabbalah can provide one with the true meaning of their being and the knowledge necessary for their ultimate benefit. It can show one spirituality that is beyond belief. The Research Centre of Kabbalah will continue to make available the Kabbalah to all those who seek it.

—Rav Berg, 1984

About The Zohar

The Zohar, the basic source of the Kabbalah, was authored two thousand years ago by Rabbi Shimon bar Yochai while hiding from the Romans in a cave in Peki'in for 13 years. It was later brought to light by Rabbi Moses de Leon in Spain, and further revealed through the Safed Kabbalists and the Lurianic system of Kabbalah.

The programs of the Research Centre of Kabbalah have been established to provide opportunities for learning, teaching, research, and demonstration of specialized knowledge drawn from the ageless wisdom of the Zohar and the Jewish sages. Long kept from the masses, today this knowledge of the Zohar and Kabbalah should be shared by all who seek to understand the deeper meaning of this spiritual heritage, and a deeper and more profound meaning of life. Modern science is only beginning to discover what our sages veiled in symbolism. This knowledge is of a very practical nature and can be applied daily for the betterment of our lives and of humankind.

Darkness cannot prevail in the presence of Light. Even a darkened room must respond to the lighting of a candle. As we share this moment together we are beginning to witness, and indeed some of us are already participating in, a people's revolution of enlightenment. The darkened clouds of strife and conflict will make their presence felt only as long as the Eternal Light remains concealed.

The Zohar now remains an ultimate, if not the only, solution to infusing the cosmos with the revealed Lightforce of the Creator. The Zohar is not a book about religion. Rather, the Zohar is concerned with the relationship between the unseen forces of the cosmos, the Lightforce, and the impact on humanity.

The Zohar promises that with the ushering in of the Age of Aquarius, the cosmos will become readily accessible to human understanding. It states that in the days of the Messiah "there will no longer be the necessity for one to request of his neighbor, teach me wisdom." (Zohar, Naso 9:65) "One day, they will no longer teach every man his neighbor and every man his brother, saying know the Lord. For they shall all know Me, from the youngest to the oldest of them." (Jeremiah 31:34)

We can, and must, regain dominion of our lives and environment. To achieve this objective, the Zohar provides us with an opportunity to transcend the crushing weight of universal negativity.

The daily perusing of the Zohar, without any attempt at translation or understanding will fill our consciousness with the Light, improving our well-being, and influencing all in our environment toward positive attitudes. Even the scanning of the Zohar by those unfamiliar with the Hebrew *Alef Bet* will accomplish the same result.

The connection that we establish through scanning the Zohar is one of unity with the Light of the Creator. The letters, even if we do not consciously know Hebrew or Aramaic, are the channels through which the connection is made and can be likened to dialing the right telephone number or typing in the right codes to run a computer program. The connection is established at the metaphysical level of our being and radiates into our physical plane of existence. But first there is the prerequisite of metaphysical "fixing." We have to consciously, through positive thought and actions, permit the immense power of the Zohar to radiate love, harmony, and peace into our lives for us to share with all humanity and the universe.

As we enter the years ahead, the Zohar will continue to be a people's book, striking a sympathetic chord in the hearts and minds of those who long for peace, truth, and relief from suffering. In the face of crises and catastrophe, the Zohar has the ability to resolve agonizing human afflictions by restoring each individual's relationship with the Lightforce of the Creator.

—Rav Berg, 1984

Kabbalah Centre Books

72 Names of God, The: Technology for the Soul

72 Names of God for Kids, The: A Treasury of Timeless Wisdom

72 Names of God Meditation Book, The

And You Shall Choose Life: An Essay on Kabbalah, the Purpose of Life, and Our True Spiritual Work

Angel Intelligence: How Your Consciousness Determines Which Angels Come Into Your Life

AstrologiK: Kabbalistic Astrology Guide for Children

Becoming Like God: Kabbalah and Our Ultimate Destiny

Beloved of My Soul: Letters of Our Master and Teacher Rav Yehuda Tzvi Brandwein to His Beloved Student Kabbalist Rav Berg

Consciousness and the Cosmos (Previously Star Connection)

Days of Connection: A Guide to Kabbalah's Holidays and New Moons

Days of Power Part 1

Days of Power Part 2

Dialing God: Daily Connection Book

Education of a Kabbalist

Energy of the Hebrew Letters, The (Previously Power of the Aleph Beth Vols. 1 and 2)

Finding the Light Through the Darkness: Inspirational Lessons Rooted in the Bible and the Zohar

God Wears Lipstick: Kabbalah for Women

Holy Grail, The: A Manifesto on the Zohar

If You Don't Like Your Life, Change It!: Using Kabbalah to Rewrite the Movie of Your Life

Immortality: The Inevitability Of Eternal Life

Kabbalah Connection, The: Preparing the Soul For Pesach

Kabbalah for the Layman

Kabbalah Method, The: The Bridge Between Science and the Soul, Physics and Fulfillment, Quantum and the Creator

Kabbalah on the Sabbath: Elevating Our Soul to the Light

Kabbalah: The Power To Change Everything

Kabbalistic Astrology: And the Meaning of Our Lives

Kabbalistic Bible: Genesis

Kabbalistic Bible: Exodus

Kabbalistic Bible: Leviticus

Kabbalistic Bible: Numbers

Kabbalistic Bible: Deuteronomy

Life Rules: How Kabbalah Can Turn Your Life From a Problem into a Solution

Living Kabbalah

Light of Wisdom: On Wisdom, Life, and Eternity